DESPERATE
HOUSELIES

S A L L Y **M A R C E Y**

Multnomah® Publishers *Sisters, Oregon*

DESPERATE HOUSE LIES

published by Multnomah Publishers, Inc.

© 2006 by The Livingstone Corporation
International Standard Book Number: 1-59052-743-7

Project staff includes:
Linda Taylor, Betsy Schmitt, Diane Stortz, Linda DeVries , Christopher Hudson,
Pastor Neil Wilson, M.A.R., Graham Barker. Psy.D., Rev. Thomas G. Britton, M.S.,
Pastor, Lynn Cirigliano, Joan L. Guest, MSW, LCSW, Kent Keller

Cover design by The DesignWorks Group, Inc.
Cover image by Steve Gardner, www.shootpw.com

Unless otherwise indicated, Scripture quotations are from:
The Holy Bible, New International Version (NIV) © 1973, 1984 by International Bible
Society. Used by permission of Zondervan Publishing House.

Other Scripture quotations are from:
The Holy Bible, King James Version (KJV).
The Holy Bible, New Living Translation (NLT), © 1996, 2004. Used by permission of
Tyndale House Publishers, Inc., Wheaton, Illinois 60189. All rights reserved.
The New American Standard Bible (NASB), © 1960, 1962, 1963, 1968, 1971, 1972,
1973, 1975, 1977, 1995. Used by permission of The Lockman Foundation.
The New King James Version (NKJV), © 1979, 1980, 1982 by Thomas Nelson, Inc.
Used by permission. All rights reserved.

Multnomah is a trademark of Multnomah Publishers, Inc.,
and is registered in the U.S. Patent and Trademark Office.
The colophon is a trademark of Multnomah Publishers, Inc.
Printed in the United States of America

For information:
MULTNOMAH PUBLISHERS, INC. • 601 N LARCH ST • SISTERS, OR 97759

Library of Congress Cataloging-in-Publication Data

Marcey, Sally.
Desperate house lies / Sally Marcey.
p. cm.
ISBN 1-59052-743-7
1. Sex—Religious aspects—Christianity. 2. Women—Conduct of life. 3. Women—
Religious life. I. Title.
BT708.M373 2006
241' .66—dc22

2006018143

06 07 08 09 10—10 9 8 7 6 5 4 3 2 1 0

Table of Contents

Introduction

Desperate Choices,
Desperate Lies

Lies, deception, false promises, revenge. Gabrielle married Carlos more for money and lust than for love, so she searches for someone younger to keep her feeling beautiful. Lynette was a highly successful businesswoman until she met Tom and decided to stay home with the kids. Now she's back in the working world supporting her husband and kids. Bree lived a life of perfection. Her husband Rex's adultery created a wedge between them and drew her into an "emotional affair" with the local pharmacist. Susan has worked hard to overcome the pain of her ex-husband Karl leaving her for a younger woman. Searching for love, her relationships leave her feeling insecure and rejected. Edie teases and flirts with any man nearby and often is the cause of others' marital distress.

Five women, all in different places in life but suffering from the same problem—they're looking for something more in their lives. You may recognize them as the characters on TV's *Desperate Housewives*. While the circumstances of their lives continue to cycle into made-for-TV difficulties and wrong choices, we also know that the white-picket fence perfection that we think surrounds us in our own lives or in our neighborhoods may be no more real than Wisteria Lane. Studies show that more than one-quarter of women have admitted to having at least one extramarital sexual act. More than 50 percent have struggled with "emotional infidelity."

Who are these women who have found themselves in an affair or playing on the edges of one? They may live down the street. They might attend PTA with you or sit in nearby cubicles at your office. They may attend your church or even your Bible study. Young or old. Stunning or somewhat plain. Full-time employees or stay-at-home moms. Their interests, talents, and friendships vary, but these desperate women have one thing in common—they're in the process of destroying their own marriages and probably someone else's.

How did they get here? What brought them to this place? The paths each woman took are as different as the women themselves. Some intentionally went looking for excitement. Others innocently sent signals that were misread by the men around them. Some were unhappy in their marriages and felt they deserved more. Some were in happy marriages and just weren't prepared for temptation. Others overestimated their ability to handle temptation. They all played with fire—and got burned.

Why does this happen? *How* does it happen? Many of these women are Christians. They know better. If you had asked them several years ago if they were going to have affairs, they would have stared at you with shock and responded, "Me? No way! Are you kidding?" Yet here they are. Many are hurting and broken. Some have lost everything. Some are trying to rebuild what has been broken. Some are still stubbornly trying to place the blame elsewhere rather than take responsibility for their own choices.

Even though they traveled to this place by varied routes, each woman has one thing in common: choices. Somewhere along the way, each made a conscious choice to cross a line…and then another line…and then another. Each subsequent wrong choice became easier and easier. Much has been written about why we make the choices that we make. Certainly we are shaped by our early relationships and impacted by our current environments, but we are still responsible for what we decide to do. When we choose sin, we are casualties in the war between good and evil.

I have written this book with an intentionally cosmic perspective. We as women often don't appreciate the significance of our lives and what God is doing through us day by day when we are faithful. We may not want to acknowledge it, but we are in a war. Ever since Eve chose evil and sin entered our world, a spiritual war has raged and encompassed our everyday lives and choices. By making a commitment to follow Christ, we engage in that war. And make no mistake—you and your marriage are one of the battlefields. Satan's plan is *not* for you to be faithful to God and to love your husband. Satan's desire is for you to be dissatisfied with your marriage, bored, unhappy, and susceptible to temptation.

Our enemy, the devil, is patient. His tactics are usually subtle; temptation comes in stages. He entices you to make each little choice that takes you a few steps away from the path of godliness. And then another few steps. At that point you might be seeking out others who find God's way too restrictive or "outdated." Satan knows that as you travel away from the path God has laid out for you, at some point it will take only one final step to send you sliding the rest of the way downward. "There is a way that seems right to a man, but in the end it leads to death" (Proverbs 14:12).

Wrong choices go all the way back to the first marriage—and the first woman. Eve had it all. God loved her. She knew God and

He knew her. Eve's husband loved her. There were no other women around to tempt him—and no men to tempt her! She didn't have to work for a living. They didn't have money problems or a mortgage to pay or retirement to worry about. Eve had a beautiful home that didn't need constant redecorating. She wasn't concerned about her weight. She didn't even have to worry about housework and laundry! She and Adam both had meaningful work in which to invest their gifts and talents. At the point of her sin, she was living life the way God created her to live it—surrounded by beauty in a close relationship with Him and with her husband.

But what did Eve do with perfection? She defied God and deliberately chose to disobey Him. God's provision wasn't enough for Eve. She wanted more. Sin entered the world through Eve's poor choice and daily we live with the consequences that affect every part of our lives. Even as Christians we deal with that sin; every day we face temptations and every day we make choices that affect us, our marriages, and our families.

Satan's tactics should not surprise us. We've got some pretty good clues from Scripture about how Satan operates.

QUESTION EVERYTHING

Satan likes to cause us to be discontented with what we have, question the boundaries God has set, or question if there's more to life. As we've said, Eve had it all. But Satan caused her to think that God was withholding blessings from her. Listen to the exchange:

[The serpent, Satan] said to the woman, "Did God really say, 'You must not eat from any tree in the garden'?" The woman said to the serpent, "We may eat fruit from the trees in the garden, but God did say, 'You must not eat fruit from the tree that is in the middle of the garden…or you will die.'"

"You will not surely die," the serpent said to the woman. "For God knows that when you eat of it your eyes will be opened, and you will be like God, knowing good and evil." (Genesis 3:1–5)

Eve had it all, but she wanted more. We watch in horror as she takes matters into her own hands and disobeys God. She crosses the one boundary that protected her, rather than trusting God's wisdom and guidance.

Are you currently questioning your life? Are you less than satisfied with where you are—and with the man you married? Do you want to reach for the forbidden choice, thinking that it will fulfill some aching longing in your heart? Do you think God is holding out on you, that you'll be better off if you can just take a different path? You have a choice.

YOU DESERVE THIS

Satan sometimes makes us think we've been through so much, we deserve this relationship that we want so much. Even if it's outside the boundaries, God will look the other way. On the edge of the Promised Land, Moses struck a rock with his walking staff. That seems like a minor thing. He was angry at the Israelites and fed up with their constant complaining. He'd been listening to it for years!

He and Aaron gathered the assembly together in front of the rock and Moses said to them, "Listen, you rebels, must we bring you water out of this rock?" Then Moses raised his arm and struck the rock twice with his staff. Water gushed out, and the community and their live-stock drank.

But the Lord said to Moses and Aaron, "Because you did not trust in me enough to honor me as holy in the sight of the Israelites, you will not bring this community into the land I give them." (Numbers 20:10–12)

If anyone deserved to have God excuse a disobedient choice, Moses did. He had faithfully led and interceded for the Israelites for almost forty years. But there beside the rock, he took God's place: "Must *we* bring you water...?" At that moment, Moses lost his right to enter the Promised Land. He was a leader; much was expected of him. With just one decision to defy God, he lost that longed-for privilege.

Is Satan seducing you, telling you that you deserve to step outside God's plan? You've been through so much you *deserve* more than what God has provided—so what that your desire is sinful?

This is another of Satan's lies. The truth is that when you step outside the protection of God's boundaries—no matter what your rationale for doing so—there will be consequences. Step off the path of following Christ, and the slide into sin *will* happen. The choice is yours.

WHY RESIST?

Sometimes Satan puts a temptation in our way and, because of where we are in life, we just don't have the desire or strength to resist it. King David should have been at war with his troops, but he sent them into battle and stayed home. Whether he was straying from God at the time or was feeling tired or bored or proud is unknown. What we do know is that he didn't even try to resist the temptation to sin.

> In the spring, at the time when kings go off to war, David sent Joab out with the king's men and the whole Israelite army…. But David remained in Jerusalem.
>
> One evening David got up from his bed and walked around on the roof of the palace. From the roof he saw a woman bathing. The woman was very beautiful, and David sent someone to find out about her. The man said, "Isn't this Bathsheba, the daughter of Eliam and the wife of Uriah the Hittite?" Then David sent messengers to get her. She came to him, and he slept with her…. Then she went back home (2 Samuel 11:1–4).

David knew better. We read these verses and the rest of chapter 11 and observe the downward spiral into intrigue and murder, and we wonder how this could have happened to David, a man after God's own heart. Yet it all started when he saw Bathsheba bathing and then made the choice to send someone "to find out about her." He made a choice to follow up on his desire, and the consequences reverberated for the rest of his life and throughout the lives of his children.

Are you facing a temptation right now in your life? A man you'd like to get to know better, or someone who has given all the signals that he is ready to get to know *you* better? What are you going to do? It's your choice.

As women living in a fallen world, no matter what our spiritual condition, we will be tempted. Some of the more subtle temptations will come in our relationships. As we stand for Jesus and walk in obedience, such attacks may be more pronounced and vicious. Some of the most painful attacks and temptations may come in our most intimate relationships, our marriages. We may experience rejection and betrayal and even abandonment in a variety of ways. These attacks do not necessarily mean that something is the wrong with us; instead, they may be a sign that we are being used by God to make inroads into Satan's domain.

The stories in this book were chosen to represent a number of the lies that the enemy uses to introduce temptation into our lives. What are these common lies? I have included seven in this book—although there are many more and many variations on these. Each chapter explains a particular lie in depth and includes three true stories, for a total of twenty-one true, heartbreaking stories of women who believed the lies. We gathered these stories from counselors and pastors across the country. Names have been changed and circumstances rewritten enough to make the women unrecognizable, but their stories are true. They believed one of the lies, they made a choice, and they paid dearly for it.

Throughout each chapter you'll find numerous Red Flags. Read these and be honest with yourself. After all, if you are able to identify these lies in your life *before* anything happens, you will be saving yourself, your husband, and your children a lot of heartache. That is my hope for you and one of my reasons for writing this book. A section called The Truth focuses on the realities that contradict each lie—realities grounded in the truth of God's Word. Finally, a Take Action section provides things to think about, write about, and pray about to help you take action against the lie and to strengthen you to stand for the truth.

The Bible has much to say about sexual sin. In my practice I have observed that someone currently caught up in an affair has a distorted view of reality, much as an addict does when she is using drugs or alcohol. Often it is only after a woman breaks free of the sin and repents of the affair that she is able to clearly see what she was doing and how destructive it was. When "under the influence" of this kind of sin, it seems to matter little what her belief system is, how faithful she has been in the past, or even the condition of her marriage before she was tempted.

Affairs are fundamentally disorienting. Often the change is so great that spouses wonder if they really know their partners! As Willard Harley states in his excellent book, *Surviving an Affair:*

> The truth is that infidelity doesn't necessarily develop out of a bankrupt system of moral values. Instead personal values change to accommodate the affair. What had been inconceivable prior to an affair can actually seem reasonable and even morally right after an affair. Many people who have always believed in being faithful in marriage find that their values do not protect them when they are faced with the temptation of an affair.

If you are being tempted or are already involved in an affair, know that your thoughts and feelings have already been affected. The lies I have chosen for this book demonstrate some of the common distortions that women have used to justify unfaithfulness. By reading these stories and interacting with the red flags and the questions that follow, it is my prayer that you will see the temptations of the enemy in your life and be able to resist them.

Know that if you are already caught in an affair, there is still hope. God is a God of second chances. While there are consequences for our actions, God uses our brokenness and humility as we again offer our lives to Him. And take great hope, dear one, because all in heaven watch and cheer us on!

> Therefore, since we are surrounded by such a great cloud of witnesses, let us throw off everything that hinders and the sin that so easily entangles, and let us run with perseverance the race marked out for us. Let us fix our eyes on Jesus, the author and perfecter of our faith, who for the joy set before him endured the cross, scorning its shame, and sat down at the right hand of the throne of God. Consider him who endured such opposition from sinful men, so that you will not grow weary and lose heart. (Hebrews 12:1–3)

No matter what we have done, no matter how badly we have fallen, God loves us with an everlasting love and stands ready to forgive us, to enfold us with His embrace, and to again set our feet on the path of following Him so that we may run our race for His glory. We do not run our race alone. God stands ready to help us so that we "will not grow weary and lose heart." May we find our deep strength and comfort in Him!

Lie #1

It's okay to flirt with other men. It's harmless; I'm just having fun.

Jorie was only a high school freshman when she discovered that flirting often paid off. Her English teacher had rigid rules about turning assignments in on time. But Jorie, who had matured early, found that if she sat on the teacher's desk in a short skirt, he often ignored the penalties when she turned in late papers.

As her high school career progressed, so did Jorie's ability to sense which teachers she could manipulate with a little bit of feminine charm. She knew just what to wear to appear innocent yet with a bit of mystery and sensuality. When she worked it right, flirting never failed her.

Of course, with the guys her age, flirting paid off there, too. A smile, a quick hug, a certain look in the eye, a touch—Jorie learned to use these to her advantage. She never failed to have several guys wrapped completely around her little finger. She could get them to do anything for her—from helping her with homework (they did her homework while she did her nails) to buying whatever she wanted—even to carrying out her vendettas. Sometimes Jorie's power over the opposite sex surprised even her! It amazed her how a little leg, a little cleavage, a tight shirt, or a slightly bare midriff could turn guys into puppy dogs eager to please.

Jorie's parents tried to discourage this behavior when they were aware of it. Her mom had strict rules about what she could and could not wear to school—only her mom didn't know that Jorie usually stopped off at her friend Dana's house on the way to school and changed her clothes. Off came the sweatshirt and gym shoes and on went the tight, low-cut sweater and spike heels. In a flash, she transformed herself into a diva and sauntered into school like she owned the place. The guys loved it when she poked them on her way by or made slightly provocative comments when she sat down beside them. It was no surprise that in her senior year, the yearbook gave Jorie the "Biggest Flirt" award.

In her sophomore year of college, Jorie met Ryan, a senior headed for grad school. He loved her flirting, and she was completely infatuated with him. He was everything she had ever wanted—athletic but not a jock, intelligent but not geeky. They married at the start of Jorie's junior year and lived in romantic poverty until they were both out of school and ready for jobs.

Jorie began working for an advertising firm. She enjoyed the laid-back atmosphere at the office and being surrounded by creative people. It wasn't long before she fell back into her old habit of flirting. Just like her male teachers, many of the men in the office enjoyed her flirting—and Jorie used her well-honed radar to know which men she could manipulate by flirting with them. It seemed harmless enough—silly e-mails, slightly provocative comments, a slight touch. Jorie reasoned that she was making these guys feel good, so what could be the harm? Her charms helped her get projects; she was sent on business trips and moved up the ladder to new responsibilities.

Then Bill, new to the company, became Jorie's boss. Bill was single, creative, driven, and didn't take no for an answer. He and Jorie hit it off right away. Their light banter became a staple for their relationship. It was all meant in fun—at least that's what Jorie thought.

"Hey, why don't you and I work on this project together—at my place—over drinks?" Bill would say in a mock serious, sensual tone.

"Right. You can't afford me," she'd say in return.

"I didn't know I needed to pay you separately."

She'd laugh and headed back to her desk saying, "Yeah, you wish."

RED FLAG: *Are there coworkers or friends with whom you enjoy trading sexual innuendos?* ≋

Once when no one was around, Bill put his arm around Jorie. She laughed and pushed him away, but later, when they were alone again, she put her arm around him, just to be a tease.

Bill became a bit more aggressive, promoting Jorie so he could work with her more. Jorie wanted to take on more responsibility, but it seemed that Bill was doing all the work and she was just the window dressing. Yet the pay was so good, Jorie wanted to keep the status quo. She and Ryan certainly were benefiting from her constant raises. A little flirting wasn't hurting; it was really helping...at least that's what she told herself.

Bill and Jorie often visited clients together, either driving or flying. As these trips became more frequent, the constant flirtation between them led to other things. Jorie had begun to feel the same pleasure in Bill's company that she had felt early on in her relationship with Ryan, before marriage made him more familiar. Flirting with Bill was exciting—a turn-on. Finally, on an out-of-town overnight trip, Jorie and Bill slept together in her room.

RED FLAG: *Is your behavior with men you know causing problems in your thought life?* ≣

Jorie's sexual relationship with Bill led to another big promotion—beyond her abilities, but Bill covered for her. After just a few months, however, Bill was transferred elsewhere, and Jorie's inability to fulfill the responsibilities of her job was exposed. She and Bill hadn't fooled their coworkers a bit, and when Bill was gone, Jorie was quickly fired.

She would never forget the drive home on that last day of work. She felt humiliated. She had flirted with guys all her life—how had flirting with Bill gotten so out of hand? How had she allowed herself to fall into this situation? And what was she going to tell Ryan?

She pulled into the driveway, and then sat in her car and wept. She had to tell Ryan everything, and she didn't know how he would react. She was terrified that in one day she would lose her reputation, her self-respect, her job, and her husband. ∎

JUST A LITTLE HARMLESS FUN

Advocates of flirting say that it's a harmless way to improve one's self esteem and to communicate positive feelings toward someone else. They couldn't be more wrong.

Flirting describes a wide range of behavior. Teasing, joking, and laughing with your friends who are men—these can all be called flirting. But other definitions help us see that flirting has a more serious and potentially problematic side: "playful behavior designed to arouse sexual interest" and "to behave amorously without serious intent." This kind of flirting is sexual and, as Jorie discovered, can progress from verbal teasing and innuendo to physical touch and hugs to a sexual relationship. The results can be devastating, and especially so if you are flirting with men outside of your marriage.

Above all else, flirting communicates your awareness of another person's sexuality. At entry level, flirting communicates, "I'm a woman, and I find you attractive as a man." Unfortunately, flirting is behavior that is easily misunderstood.

One woman who flirts may be sending the message, "You're an attractive man and I appreciate that, but I have no intentions of going further." Another woman's flirting may be saying, "I find you attractive and wonder if you find me attractive too? Are you interested in pursuing a relationship?" The differences in the flirting itself are real but subtle. Which message is heard may depend more on the recipient than on the person who is doing the flirting.

When you flirt, you are adding a sexual current to your communication with a man. You are sending the conflicting message that you are both sexually interested and off limits—and men can regard that as a challenge.

It's not hard to see, then, that flirting *can* have a dishonest element about it, and that's a problem. When you send a message that you find someone sexually attractive and respond to him in provocative ways, he may not realize that you have no intention of acting on the message you are sending. You are, at the core of your behavior, lying. Yet God places a high premium on honesty throughout the Bible, and Jesus said, "Simply let your 'Yes' be 'Yes,' and your 'No,' 'No' " (Matthew 5:37).

If you routinely flirt with your male colleagues or friends and you wonder about the appropriateness of your behavior, imagine that someone you respect is watching those interactions. Would you feel comfortable with this person present? How might he or she see the situation?

WHO'S IN CONTROL?

Often without realizing it, women flirt to manipulate or control relationships—to get what we want or need. But when we do this, we are looking in the wrong places for what we hope to find.

If you are married, you might feel safe in flirting. Because you're "taken," you may even feel willing to flirt *more* than you did before you were married. Let's think about why. Flirting might make you feel like you are in control and solving your problems without having to put forth much effort. Maybe you have difficulty viewing yourself as an adequate person. But rather than turn to your husband, a trusted friend, or a counselor for help with this underdeveloped aspect of your character, you take the easier route of flirting with other men to get attention and to feel more attractive and valuable. It feels like a solution, it's fun and easy, and you're in control.

Flirting is using your sexuality in a manipulative way to influence others and get something you want. But that is not why God designed us as sexual beings. He intends for our sexuality to help us express oneness with our marriage partner. The attitude toward sex found in Genesis 2:24, "A man will leave his father and mother and be united to his wife, and they will become one flesh," is reflected throughout the Bible.

Flirting also allows us to enjoy the feelings of attraction toward a man yet not own our behavior—we're not planning to *act* on those feelings. Yet we are responsible for our behavior and for how it is perceived: "So then, each of us will give an account of himself to God" (Romans 14:12).

SIREN SONG

We are rarely aware of the entire story of someone else's circumstances, and our behavior may be more of a problem for him than we realize. That coworker who appears so nonchalant and self-confident at the office could be struggling with a painful marriage or a previous job loss; he may be very susceptible to a woman's flirting because his needs for affirmation aren't being fulfilled in other ways. Flirting with any man makes you a real source of temptation to him in his thought life, even if he doesn't respond with actions.

Jesus places a high standard on our hearts and what we think about. In the Sermon on the Mount, as He taught about the Ten Commandments and the kingdom of God, Jesus said, "But I tell you that anyone who looks at a woman lustfully has already committed adultery with her in his heart" (Matthew 5:28). Later, the apostle Paul directed, "Live in such a way that you will not cause another believer to stumble and fall" (Romans 14:13, NLT)

For Jorie, flirting was a way to enjoy the feelings of attraction without having to take responsibility for her behavior or, initially, to act on those feelings. The mixed message from pretending to be available while simultaneously keeping Bill at a distance challenged him, and he responded by becoming more aggressive. Jorie's behavior produced a sexual tension that eventually she couldn't handle, and the physical boundaries were crossed. She had already crossed the boundaries of sexual thoughts toward Bill long before.

Another issue for Jorie was the manipulative way she used her sexuality to get what she wanted. Unfortunately, this behavior was reinforced early in her life, and she'd experienced no negative consequences she was aware of until now. So she remained convinced her flirting was harmless, but her situation was similar to always relying on cheating to pass tests without being caught. Jorie had learned to subtly use her sexuality to influence and control others, and now, without any realistic feedback, she continued to flirt with her coworkers until her circumstances forced her to look at the results. And now she wonders how things got so out of hand with a little "harmless flirting."

MIXED MESSAGES

Communication involves what is "said" and what is "heard"— often with no words spoken at all. The message we are sending may not be the message that is being received. That can lead to a terrible result, as Carol learned in a traumatic way.

■ Carol is a vibrant, young, energetic Christian woman with a high-level career in the banking field. Newly married to an up-and-coming attorney, Carol has a painful secret in her past that has been bubbling to the surface and causing havoc in her marriage.

In high school, Carol's life had been full of friends and activities. She was always at the center of whatever was happening—whether it was school dances, or fund-raisers, or just hanging out. Wherever Carol was, there soon would be a party. It was all innocent—when they weren't studying, Carol and her friends spent evenings with popcorn and a video, making cookies and listening to music, or going to a movie or Christian concert. She made plans and everyone followed. That was just the way it was.

Carol enrolled at a state university because her parents couldn't afford to send her to one of the Christian institutions that had been at the top of her list. She thought she could handle the pressures of a secular school. She didn't want to pledge a sorority, but chose instead to live in the dorm and find other Christians on campus. During her freshman year, she stayed focused on her grades and away from the party scene.

But getting to college and trying to remain apart from so many activities began to cause Carol to feel that she was missing out on so much. The Christians she met were not the kind of people she wanted to spend lots of time with. They were...well...boring. Carol wanted some excitement in her life. She didn't want to drink and do drugs, but she wanted to get into the center of something fun. *Besides*, she thought, *I need to meet people if I'm going to impact them.* She just didn't realize how much they would end up impacting her.

When sophomore year began, Carol yearned to be a part of some of the fun activities around her. She began to let her standards slip a bit. She still doesn't know whether this happened because she felt she had been too rigid as a freshman or whether she just got tired of holding to a line that no longer seemed to matter.

Carol started going out with some of the girls she met in an exercise class. They seemed safe enough; all of them were health conscious, so they didn't drink much. Carol felt comfortable with them and spearheaded some activities, like a morning jog with a stop at Starbucks and a picnic on the dorm lawn. One Friday afternoon in the winter, one of the other girls suggested that they go to a local dance club that night. Carol decided to go along and check it out. She had taken some dance classes in high school and knew how to swing dance and do some Latin dance and ballroom moves. It sounded like a fun night out.

She was right. The dance club was fantastic. The girls caught the eyes of a few of the college guys who also frequented the club and made their way onto the floor to dance with them. The girls watched in awe as Carol deftly did dance moves with various partners who also knew the steps. Carol felt on top of the world.

The dance club became a regular activity. Carol bought herself a couple of new dresses just for the club, slinky with just the right cut to move with the music. New strappy shoes finished off her outfits. Every week she and her friends dressed up and headed out to the club.

One night Gil joined Carol on the dance floor. She had seen him on campus and had noticed him at the club several times. He was an incredible dancer. He knew all the right moves so that together they could swing (complete with spins and tosses) and do some ballroom too (complete with dips). For laughs, they even did a tango across the room, with Carol wrapping her leg around Gil and being carried across the floor. Both of them vamped it up, to the great enjoyment of the watching crowd.

From then on, Carol and Gil danced together every week. Carol never thought about the sensuality that was part of her dancing. The heat, the lights, the music combined to make her feel different than she'd ever felt before.

RED FLAG: *Are you using physical touch in your opposite-sex relationships in inappropriate ways?* ≋

One night, Gil and Carol lingered after everyone else left. They continued to dance together and then sat for a while as Gil had another beer. Carol offered to drive Gil home since he'd had so much to drink, and he took her up on it. Gil wanted to come up to Carol's room, and Carol didn't really want him to leave, so though it was late, Carol brought him into her room to watch some TV.

Gil closed the door and then laughingly grabbed Carol as if to continue dancing. Carol laughed and Gil pulled her closer. She enjoyed his attention, his arms around her, his kisses on her lips, but she realized she hardly knew him. Carol liked feeling sexy on the dance floor, but to her, that was all it was—dancing. The caresses and kissing continued, but when Carol wanted Gil to stop, he wouldn't. Instead, he raped her.

Although she begged him to stop, he refused. "You've been leading me on all night," he said. "You can't turn me off like a light switch." When it was over, he left her. When he saw her again, he acted as if nothing had happened.

Carol never reported the rape. Eventually she was tested for STDs. The results were all negative, but the rape changed her life forever.

RED FLAG: *Are you keeping a secret that is causing you shame or guilt?* ≋

Carol has kept this secret for years. Now that she's married, the pain and the shame seem especially acute. She had always planned to stay a virgin until she got married. Except for the rape, she had done so. Still she can't shake the feeling that she needs to tell her husband what happened, but she doesn't know what to say. It was all just silly, sensual, flirtatious dancing—nothing more... ■

Carol flirted not only with Gil, but in her innocence, she was flirting with danger. Perhaps her interactions with men who had respected her and treated her well in the past had not prepared her for someone like Gil, and so she put herself at risk. She didn't know him well, she invited him up to her room after he had been drinking, and she enjoyed being sexually provocative with him, yet she assumed he would respect her boundaries.

The importance of keeping good boundaries as a way of protecting oneself rather than giving over that responsibility to someone else is key. Carol would not have left valuable heirloom jewelry lying about where it could be stolen or damaged, but she treated *herself* as if she were expendable instead of priceless. Naively assuming safety when we are actually at risk is a foolish choice.

Yet rape is a crime of violence, and "date rape" is still rape, no matter what behavior on the part of the victim precedes the act. Flirting may send messages that a woman is willing to have sex, but forcing sex on her, regardless of her behavior, is still rape.

Carol did not report the rape, probably because she felt confused about what led up to it. Her flirting put her at risk, and now it is causing confusion, guilt, and inability to take action. She's neglecting herself emotionally instead of coming forward to get the care she needs.

To be raped is to be traumatized. Carol needs professional help to deal with the rape and the guilt she feels and to regain her sense of well-being and safety.

NOT WHAT IT SEEMS

■ Sometimes the reasons women flirt are not what we tell ourselves or others. Sometimes the result of flirting is not at all what it seems. That's what Peggy discovered.

Peggy and Jack dated in high school and college and had not known any other serious relationships in their lives. Now Peggy is a young wife and mother with a lucrative career in sales, a job that requires her to spend many weekends away from home at conventions and client meetings across the country.

Peggy loves her job. She is a people person, completely energized by being with new people, meeting potential clients at conventions, entertaining clients, and sitting down with them in their own office settings in order to really get to know them well. But she tries to keep her trips short so that she's not gone from her "boys" for very long—refer-ring to her twin sons and her husband, Jack.

At the office, Peggy is at the center of everything that goes on. Since she's the key salesperson, she's depended on to make the face-to-face contact, represent the company in a positive way, build trust, and make the sale. Her vivacious personality allows her to do just that. Clients enjoy talking to Peggy. She remembers their names, the names of their spouses and children, and other details that make the clients feel important. Because Peggy is so talkative and friendly, she's also very popular among her coworkers, who are mostly men.

Peggy loves her husband, but Jack is not very comfortable with the men at his wife's office. He knows Peggy is very friendly and that she is a person who touches and hugs, but at the first office party he went to with her, he was surprised at how much she talked and touched and hugged her male coworkers. He confronted her about it.

"Peggy, what's going on with all those men at your office? I felt re-ally uncomfortable at that party tonight, like I was the odd man out. I mean, all these inside jokes, and I think every man in the room hugged you. And you didn't seem to mind."

RED FLAG: *Is your husband complaining or expressing concern about your flirting with men at work, at church, or in the neighborhood?* ≣

"Jack, come on. You don't need to worry about these guys, believe me. I'm sorry you felt uncomfortable. I'm with these guys at least nine hours a day. We're just buddies."

"Well, those guys act real uncomfortable around me, like they're guilty or something."

"So, do you think I'm having an affair? Please, give me some credit! I love you. We've got two boys to take care of. I just do what I need to do to survive at work and keep bringing in the money we need!"

But Jack couldn't shake the feeling. He started dropping by Peggy's office once in a while to take her to lunch. Peggy was always glad to see him—but often seemed surprised or distracted. Sometimes she already had a lunch meeting planned with one of those male coworkers. Jack became more and more uncomfortable. When Peggy left for her frequent business trips, Jack wondered if he could trust her. He hated feeling that way. Maybe he trusted Peggy, but he didn't trust her coworkers. That's when he sought out a marriage counselor. After a frank discussion with the counselor, he agreed to ask Peggy to come with him to a subsequent session.

Peggy was very open with the counselor—her talkative and vivacious self. But she was angry that Jack was being so suspicious. "I have nothing to hide," she repeated over and over. "I haven't done anything I'm ashamed of."

Jack continued to insist that she was acting in an inappropriate and flirtatious manner with her coworkers. "I'm not being a flirt!" Peggy responded.

"Well, maybe you don't think so, but I saw the looks in the eyes of those guys, I think they think you are flirting."

The counselor asked Peggy to describe the nature of the flirting.

"Well, I've always been friendly with the people around me. Yes, I do touch and hug, but it means nothing. And I guess there is a lot of innuendo. That really started back when I got pregnant. I got big fast because of the twins, so there were all kinds of jokes about my size, about conception versus contraception, about my husband's virility. I decided that either I'd have to be the butt of the jokes or stake my ground and give it back to them. I never talked about sex or about Jack in that way, but these guys were always finding a sexual side to anything I said. I've just learned to toss it back at them and play the game. Keeps me from being a victim and maintains my power position. I usually get a good laugh from the rest of the guys when I've really gotten back at one of them.

RED FLAG: *What is your reputation at work? Can your coworkers depend upon you for a sexual joke or innuendo?* ≋

"But maybe it was going too far. I mean, one of our running jokes has always been to pretend like affairs are going on. One guy will pretend he's having a tryst with the aged secretary to the president. Another will pretend he's got something going with the new intern. And this one guy and I often do the same; we pretend we're having an affair just to get a rise out of the other guys. They know perfectly well it isn't true. For instance, if he and I have to go on a business trip, he'll ask me if I want to share a room in order to save the company money. And I'll say, 'Of course, and this time our hotel room will be covered by the company.' Stuff like that. Everyone laughs. It's just a joke."

But Jack wasn't laughing. This revelation surprised him—he hadn't realized that the little bit of flirting that bothered him was really far more intense than he had thought. He couldn't understand why Peggy didn't see this as inappropriate.

Peggy slowly began to see that she flirted because of the excitement it created to play on the edge of the cliff. She admitted that Jack loved her and that he was a good man with a kind and tender heart, but she didn't feel his passion to the degree that met her desires. She had never had another serious relationship with any man other than Jack—hadn't she missed out on something? Couldn't she experience what she had missed in a playacting way—a way she considered harmless but still felt good? She never intended for anyone to take her up on it.

In fact, Peggy realized, she wished that she and Jack flirted like that once in a while… ∎

One of the warning signs that flirting has crossed the line is a loving husband's discomfort with your behavior. Often a husband senses that something is not right before he realizes why, and his jealousy and concern are often effective indicators that behavior has gotten out of hand. Jack's concerned, appropriate, and caring response served as a restraint that protected Peggy from more serious consequences of her actions.

Jack's presence at the company party and his drop-in visits to the office were both wise actions; they communicated to Peggy's coworkers that her husband was a very real part of her life, and they allowed Jack to gain a better sense of what was happening with Peggy at work. Workplaces often include a culture of inside stories and shared experiences but cross a line when spouses are intentionally excluded.

Peggy's flirting was not only verbal; she also used physical touch in her relationships with her coworkers. Hugs and touch are meant to communicate care and warmth, but touch can be easily misunderstood by the other person. The concern is not only what you are communicating with a hug but also what the man on the receiving end of the hug experiences.

The line between warm and friendly and sexually flirtatious may seem difficult to discern at times, but it is a very important boundary to maintain in a workplace. Peggy used sexual innuendo and jokes with sexual themes to create a bond between herself and her male coworkers. Their embarrassment around Jack could be an indicator that they perceive her behavior as inappropriate, even though they participate in it.

Peggy maintained that she was using her sexual flirting to get along better in her job, but the result could actually be the opposite. How coworkers respond to one another at the office may not indicate how they actually feel. Male colleagues may go along with a woman's flirting while privately thinking that she isn't very serious about her job. Flirting may bring immediate attention and enjoyment but often undermines respect. Was Peggy known as a competent professional or as the office flirt?

Peggy was surprised to learn that her flirting grew out of her unmet needs. She longed for more passion and adventure than her marriage provided, and she has been filling in the gaps with flirting, creating a fantasy life. This puts Peggy potentially at risk with her coworkers, but equally or more important—it also *covers up* the needs in her life that are not being met and so prevents her from discovering why and then making changes. Flirting actually provides an escape for Peggy, from her marriage *and* from herself. When someone like Peggy actually stops the flirting and looks deeply at the needs that drive it, she is often surprised at the depth of pain and lack of self-worth she discovers. But that discovery is where healing starts!

THE TRUTH

It's easy to focus on the behaviors in our lives (or even in the lives of those around us) that are concerning or even sinful yet miss the deeper issues of the heart. Jorie, Carol, and Peggy all used their sexuality to gain attention, to feel good about themselves, and to manipulate or control relationships. Just stopping the flirting would be a healthy move for them. But the deeper issues in their lives will remain unless they are willing to look *within,* at the reasons they do what they do, and work on those.

Jesus was clear that our faith is not about impression management but is instead about the condition of our hearts. His harshest criticism was always for the Pharisees, religious leaders who looked good on the outside like "whitewashed tombs" (Matthew 23:27). He said, "On the outside you appear to people as righteous but on the inside you are full of hypocrisy and wickedness" (v. 28). Faith is not a set of dos and don'ts. If we think that it is, we can get into real trouble in our relationships. We might dress modestly and behave properly but inside be filled with envy and anger. It's quite possible to "look good" on the outside and even feel self-righteous about our behavior but be in real trouble in our hearts.

Conversely, Jesus showed great compassion to women who had sinned sexually but came to Him for wisdom and for forgiveness. He revealed the truth of their lives *and* He responded with grace. One example of this twofold message is Jesus' encounter with the woman at the well. Jesus named the sin in her life when He told her she had had five husbands and was currently living with someone who wasn't her husband. Then He told her about the living water that He provided. Jesus did not respond to this woman's sin with condemnation but with truth and grace, intended to lead her to repentance (see John 4:4–26).

In a similar way, when the Pharisees brought a woman caught in adultery before Jesus, He acknowledged the seriousness of her sin but reminded her accusers that they also had sin in their own lives. "If any of you is without sin, let him be the first to throw a stone at her" (John 8:7). One by one, all the men left. Then Jesus said, "Woman, where are they? Has no one condemned you?... Neither do I condemn you.... Go now and leave your life of sin" (John 8:10–11). His message to the woman was clear, and He provided a new path in which to walk.

Jesus will do the same work in our lives today if we will permit Him to do so. He will reveal to us the truth of our behavior and set us on a new path. Trying to remove problematic behaviors in our lives without restoring our relationship with Him is like pulling weeds without planting anything in their place. We can become vigilant weed-pullers yet never enjoy a harvest of flowers or fresh vegetables!

We were created to experience the power, joy, and beauty of a deep relationship with the lover of our souls. The vitality and excitement of a woman's life flows from her deep relationship with the Lord and her awareness of herself as His precious and beautiful child. Behavior that matches this awareness and commitment flows from a love relationship of the heart.

One of the most beautiful images in Scripture is of Christians as the bride of Christ (see 2 Corinthians 11:2). As the bride, the Scripture also tells us that we are radiant (see Ephesians 5:27).Our beauty truly glows from the inside out! We are His, designed for relationship with Him. How we relate with others in our marriages, friendships, and business relationships needs to be compatible with this most important relationship of our lives.

Is flirting harmless? No, it's not. Flirting involves being dishonest in communication, choosing to manipulate, and placing temptation in another's way as well as our own. Satan often doesn't require much of a foothold in our lives to begin to erode our thought life and moral resolve. "Playful" flirting easily provides an entry into our lives that will leave us vulnerable to Satan's attack. We need to be vigilant against the snares of the evil one, guarding our hearts and our lives and not giving the enemy any place to stand (see Ephesians 6:10–13).

take action

✓ Spend some time in prayer asking God to shine His
light on the relationships in your life. Invite Him
to be a loving observer as together you review the
ways you relate to men. What do you discover?

✓ Do you see yourself as Christ's bride? How might you
strengthen your love relationship with Him?

✓ Do you flirt with your husband? Are there additional
ways you can show him that you find him attractive?

✓ Flirting often provides a woman with perceived
power in a situation. If that is your experience,
ask yourself why you need that power.

✓ If there are insecurities in your life that flirting might be
compensating for, decide how you will address those.

✓ Flirting can provide a sense of adventure and excitement
if those are lacking in your life. Take some time to talk
with your husband about ways the two of you can
restore that excitement to your own relationship.

✓ Someone who indulges in flirting becomes known
as a flirt. Take some time and determine how you
would like to be known. Decide how you will
interact with others in ways that honor Christ.

Lie #2

Sexual freedom is good for women.

Bonnie grew up in a home with parents who believed in "open marriage"—marriage was for convenience and for the kids, but came with no restrictions. While her mom and dad never talked to her about it, in her teenage years Bonnie began to understand what was going on. Her parents' philosophy was: "It's okay to fool around. After all, people have needs."

It didn't bother Bonnie that much—she just didn't think about it. Her parents seemed happy and they stayed married. She had plenty of other things in her teenage life to keep her busy: boyfriends, school activities, boyfriends, hanging out, boyfriends, shopping, boyfriends, dinners and dances with her parents' country-club friends and their teenage kids. Her family attended church sometimes, but for them it was like another social club.

Bonnie had her first sexual encounter when she was fifteen—with her sixteen-year-old boyfriend. Her parents had given her condoms to carry in her purse so she would always be prepared. Bonnie dated more than her share of guys in high school and college and had sexual relationships with most of them.

Bonnie's dad made a great living, and her mom worked because she wanted to. Bonnie never had to work during high school; her parents were happy to give her a car on her sixteenth birthday and credit cards for whatever she wanted to purchase. They paid for her college education too. However, they weren't thrilled when Bonnie brought Al home from college—he worked in construction, after all! But Al was kind and attentive, and he would be able to provide for Bonnie in the way she was accustomed—his company specialized in the construction of high-rise buildings, difficult work with long hours but excellent pay and benefits. Bonnie's parents agreed to the marriage.

Al wanted Bonnie to have everything he could provide. They bought a nice home, a second car, and a health club membership. Bonnie was able to fill her days with shopping, working out with her personal trainer, tanning at the salon, and having lunches out with her girlfriends. Al's hours were long, but the overtime pay was excellent. Al was hard working and dependable. When he wasn't at work, he was at home. He loved yard work, maintained the home, even took out the trash without being asked!

This was fine for the first few years of their marriage, but then Bonnie began to get restless. Al's long hours didn't make it easy for Bonnie and Al to find time to spend together. Bonnie wanted to take cruises and trips, but Al either couldn't get away or wasn't interested. Al's work was stressful and active, and he came home at night extremely tired, interested only in dinner and TV. Bonnie began feeling less and less desired and fulfilled.

RED FLAG: *Is your sexual relationship with your husband unsatisfying, either to him or to you?* ≡

That's when Bonnie ran into an old boyfriend from high school at her health club. They were thrilled to see each other. Tim also was married, but it didn't take long for him to rekindle a sexual relationship with Bonnie.

Bonnie had no qualms about this. After all, she thought, I've got needs. Apparently Tim did too...and Bonnie had no qualms about helping to meet them. With Al gone all day, Bonnie and Tim met at her home.

Al was deeply wounded when he found out about the affair (through a coworker whose wife frequented the same health club and had seen the sparks flying between Bonnie and Tim). Al had thought his marriage was just fine. When he discovered Bonnie's infidelity, he felt like he'd been hit by a wrecking ball.

But when Al confronted Bonnie about the affair, her response was nonchalant. "It's no big deal," she told him. "It's just sex. Once it's over, he goes home to his wife, and you come home to me. People do it all of the time. I love you, but I need more. You're always so tired, and I feel guilty asking you for sex. If you can't live with this arrangement, maybe we should go our separate ways. I love you, but this has nothing to do with love."

Al loved Bonnie and couldn't imagine being unfaithful to her. His pain over the affair distracted him at work, making him a danger to himself and his coworkers. His boss ordered him to get some help and referred him to a counselor.

At the first session, the counselor asked Al what he wanted as the outcome of the situation. Without hesitation, Al blurted, "I love my wife more than life itself. I couldn't bear losing her. What do I do?" In response the counselor began working with Al on some of the issues that had played into Bonnie's infidelity. Then she recommended that Al ask Bonnie about coming together for counseling. Bonnie reluctantly agreed, and they began walking the long road toward reconciliation and the restoration of their marriage.

SEXUAL "FREEDOM"?

In *The Case for Marriage*, authors Linda Waite and Maggie Gallagher review research that investigated sexual activity and satisfaction within marriage. They found that sexual satisfaction for married women, both in frequency and in pleasure, is far greater than among single or divorced women. "Over the long run," they wrote, "there is no better strategy for achieving great sex than binding oneself to an equally committed mate." Their conclusion: "Married sex is better sex!"

God is very clear that sex is a part of His design to join a man and a woman together into a one-flesh union. Genesis 2:24 says, "This explains why a man leaves his father and mother and is joined to his wife, and the two are united into one" (NLT). God designed this union to take place within marriage, not to restrict us from pleasure or fulfilled desire, but to *protect* us. We are integrated beings, and the way we think and act with our bodies impacts our emotions and our souls. The writer of Proverbs tells us that as a person "thinks within himself, so he is" (Proverbs 23:7, NASB).

Sexual freedom says that anything goes whether we're married or single and that no one gets hurt by the sexual choices individuals make. "Sexual freedom is good for women" is a lie because clearly women do get hurt—and so do others around them—when they disregard the principle of keeping sexual activity within marriage. Sex before marriage, sex outside of marriage, unsatisfying marital relationships that are allowed to languish for years without looking for God's help and direction—the consequences include broken relationships between loved ones, battered self-esteem, children deprived of secure family relationships, unwanted pregnancies, interrupted dreams, disease, and a broken relationship with God.

RED FLAG: *Are you and your husband unable to have conversations about your sexual life?* ≋

Sexual "freedom" is a misnomer. One of the images for sexual passion in the Bible is "fire" or "burning with passion" (see 1 Corinthians 7:9). Fire can heat and warm and glow and ignite. We enjoy a fire in the fireplace in the winter or at a campsite on a starlit summer night. Although we are able to start a fire anywhere we wish, to start a fire in the middle of our living room or in the woods beyond the campfire would be pure foolishness.

The igniting of human sexual passion is a similar process. In a marriage, such passion serves to draw two people together and provides fulfillment and joy. By design, sexual passion focuses on the one who is loved and on ourselves in relationship to the one we love. The world is shut out in those moments! Recall the way that young lovers look at each other, as if they are the only two people who exist.

Outside of marriage, such a fire of passion causes destruction. But those who start sexual fires outside marriage often cannot see the destruction they are causing until the damage is well underway. Sexual "freedom" is really the freedom to destroy. The writer of Proverbs asks, "Can a man scoop fire into his lap without his clothes being burned?" (Proverbs 6:27).

The expression of our sexuality is a powerful gift and a

passionate fire, intended to be ignited within a marriage. We don't have the freedom to cause damage to ourselves or to others in any manner, including our sexuality. Instead, the freedom that Christ gives us is meant to be used for our good and the good of others. "For you have been called to live in freedom.... But don't use your freedom to satisfy your sinful nature. Instead, use your freedom to serve one another in love" (Galatians 5:13, NLT).

ACTIONS HAVE POWER

Starting a sexual fire outside your marriage never helps your marriage; nor is it "no big deal" where your sexual desires are fulfilled.

Adultery or any other kind of marital unfaithfulness is always a choice. We choose where we start our fires. Unhappiness or unmet needs in a marriage are never an excuse for adultery. Sometimes the betrayed husband is unfairly blamed for causing the affair because he failed to meet his wife's need for intimacy and connection. Husbands must assume responsibility for their part in whatever led to a wife's affair, but wives also are responsible for the choices they make when faced with an inattentive husband. While unmet desires in a marriage make you vulnerable to attention from outside your marriage, beginning a relationship with another man is always a choice *you* have made—it is never inevitable!

Our actions have power. Many marriages, even most marriages, go through periods of turmoil and unhappiness. Husbands and wives can choose to remain faithful to each other during the difficult times. The reward of such a choice is often a marriage relationship that is richer, stronger, and more passionate than either husband or wife imagined could be possible.

Infidelity doesn't have to end a marriage. Even though Jesus spoke about adultery as an allowable cause for divorce, divorce is not inevitable. Jesus' words to the woman who was accused of adultery still ring true today: "Go and sin no more" (John 8:11, NLT). When both husband and wife are willing to enter a process where the affair is ended permanently, the reasons for the affair are understood, and healing choices are made, the marriage can be rebuilt.

Once an affair takes place and is discovered, couples sometimes want to quickly forgive each other and move on, but it is very important to understand the meaning of the affair. David Carder, in his book and workbook *Torn Asunder*, offers a comprehensive ninety-day program for working through marital unfaithfulness. Seeking professional help after an affair helps the couple manage their emotions, process the affair, and set a course for healing.

IT MATTERS WHO YOU KNOW

Our background greatly influences our choices, so it's important to examine how our family of origin functioned and what we learned growing up there.

We learn about marriage from our parents, even if they never discuss their specific views with us. Their actions form a blueprint that becomes a part of who we are, even though we may not be aware of it. We all enter marriage with a blueprint from our parents that encompasses all aspects of marriage, including their understanding of marital sexual activity. If the model we are given doesn't include shared passion and commitment between two people within marriage only, adopting that pattern without questioning it will prove disastrous.

Just as our family of origin influences the decisions *we* make, our spiritual background influences us too. And just as the model we receive from our parents can be good or bad, the model we receive from our church-related experiences can also have a positive or a negative effect. Some women who have been raised in the church often know about God but do not have a relationship with Him. Others make commitments to Jesus as Savior but neglect to grow in their understanding of what it means to call Him Lord.

RED FLAG: *Are you trying to navigate life without a relationship with the God who created you?* ≋

In the Bible we get to know God—who He is, what He loves and what He hates, and why. He's the Creator, so He better than anyone else knows how life works, and He's told us everything we need to know to live life successfully, including how to handle our sexuality. It's all in His Word.

Without knowing God and understanding what He says about how we should live, we have only the context of our family of origin and our culture to help us make our decisions. But the family we come from may have been dysfunctional, and our culture worships the idol of self, so neither one is a reliable guide. It's up to us to question what we have learned and what we see lived out around us, then to search for what is true.

In the Bible we can discover the single most important thing we need to know to live a good life, and it's not a principle but a person—it's God Himself. Knowing God, not just knowing a few things about Him, is what can keep us on an even keel during good times and bad.

Sometimes it's the difficulties in our marriage relationships that God uses to call us back to Himself and to take us down a new path of growth with Him. Getting to know God through the Bible will certainly be part of that growth. The answers to our dilemmas often lie in our submission to God and His ways, but it's hard to submit to someone you don't know well and don't trust. Make a decision to seek out a good plan for reading the Bible to get to know God. It can make a huge difference, keeping you from bad choices and helping you deal with the consequences of bad choices you've already made.

Bonnie's willingness to see a counselor with Al was a hopeful sign for the marriage, as was Al's willingness to follow his boss's direction to get help.

Bonnie had a great deal to learn—about herself, about God, about life. She needed to understand that her confusion about sex came from her parents' lifestyle of open marriage and their approval of her sexual activity in high school and college. As Bonnie talked about her parents' relationship, she began to see that what might have appeared to be a workable relationship really was full of stress and distrust.

Bonnie had been given some exposure to the church, but she only had a bit of knowledge about God, not a relationship with Him. She didn't have a clue that she was committing adultery, that it was wrong, and that it was extremely painful for Al. In the beginning she couldn't understand why Al was so upset about her liaisons with Tim. Fortunately, she too wanted to save the marriage, and Al's willingness to examine his part in the affair right from the beginning—rather than place all the blame on her—greatly softened her heart. When the counselor suggested that Al and Bonnie begin to read the Bible and attend church together, Bonnie was willing to try. Before long, both Bonnie and Al had committed their lives to Jesus and recommitted themselves to their marriage and to each other.

Bonnie also learned to take responsibility to get her own wants and needs met *within her marriage*. She learned how to communicate to Al that she was missing him and feeling vulnerable to the attentions of another man rather than turning to that other man to meet her needs.

Fortunately, this story has a happy ending—thanks to two people willing to work on their marriage, to face the truth, and to recommit their lives to each other. The only reservation Al had was unwillingness to sleep in the bed where Tim and Bonnie had been. The solution: a new bed!

WHEN GOD SAYS NO

Married women are not the only ones who struggle with issues of sexual freedom. Single women who want to follow God's plan also need to decide whether they will trust God to provide for their well-being even when it is difficult, as this story about Lisa illustrates.

■ Lisa has always believed that "the Father knows best" concerning relationships, and she has trusted God to provide His best for her. In recent years, however, such certainties have taken some hits.

Lisa is forty-eight years old and has never been married. This causes her much sadness. When she was young, Lisa dreamed of meeting a nice guy in college, getting married, and starting a family. She had a few serious relationships in college, but none of them led to marriage. After graduation she found her first job, got her own apartment, and began living life as a single. Today she works for a large corporation, and her career is important to her. She has many good friendships and enjoys her life, but she feels that something is missing. If her plans had worked out, she would by now have kids starting college themselves. She doesn't want to be one of those women who think marriage is the only thing that can make them happy, but she can't deny that marriage is a true desire of her heart.

Lisa's feelings have always intensified at family gatherings. Thanksgiving, Christmas, weddings of cousins and friends were all times she had to steel herself against the inevitable.

RED FLAG: *Do you feel sorry for single people? Do you view singleness as a negative?*

"There's someone out there for you, my dear," said Aunt Cindy.

"So when you gonna get hitched?" asked Uncle Fred.

"I can't understand why some guy hasn't snagged you yet!" from cousin Don.

"Well, I just haven't met the right guy yet," Lisa would say with a smile.

"But you're not getting any younger, you know," Grandma Joan always replied.

Lisa was very aware of the passing of time. She would be fifty soon—"over the hill." She began to settle into the fact that she would probably never marry. The single Christian men she knew were... well... there were good reasons that they were almost fifty and still single! Lisa desperately hoped she didn't come across as needy or weird as she thought most of them did.

Although Lisa still believed that God meant sex to be for marriage only, as she grew older, her desire for intimacy seemed to grow stronger. She limited the suggestive movies, TV shows, and music she watched or listened to, but still it was easy to conclude that everybody except her had someone to love. It was also easy to get the message that sex outside marriage was really no big deal, that women were expected to go after what they desired, that being with a sexually aggressive woman was something men enjoyed—and even expected—in a dating relationship.

Steve was transferred to Lisa's office from another branch of her company. Steve was different from the other men in the office and from most of the single Christian guys Lisa knew. Not only was he not threatened by her intelligence and accomplishments, he seemed to genuinely appreciate them. Lisa noted with interest that there was no ring on his left hand.

Steve asked Lisa to join him for lunch at the end of his first week. She was intrigued and delighted by his attention. He never mentioned a wife or children... and Lisa did not inquire about them. He did mention looking for a church.

About a month later, Steve and Lisa stayed late at the office to work on a project. They took a dinner break and ordered in; when the food was delivered, they headed to the empty staff lounge. They talked and laughed while they ate. One casual touch on the arm led to another, and soon Lisa longed to kiss him.

Working late together soon became Saturday afternoons at Lisa's apartment. Their physical relationship grew, and Lisa became completely obsessed with Steve. She loved the closeness she felt with him. Somewhere deep inside she felt a twinge of guilt, but she always pushed it aside. I need this, she told herself. I'm deeply in love and we'll surely get married—at our age, why would we wait? It will all turn out fine—after all, everyone does it. And now I understand why! It seemed to Lisa that the scattered pieces of her life were finally coming together in this handsome man.

Nobody else in the office knew of their relationship. There was no prohibition on dating coworkers as long as neither supervised the other, but they had agreed to keep things quiet. Their "little secret" certainly added to the excitement. However, the office Christmas party was coming up, and Lisa thought it would be fun to make their relationship known.

"That's impossible!" Steve said.

"But why?" Lisa wanted to know. "It's not against policy here. Besides, I want everyone to know! My family wants to meet you too! We can start making holiday plans."

"My wife will be at the office Christmas party," Steve said quietly.

Lisa was stunned. "Your wife? You never said anything about being married!"

"You never asked, so I assumed you knew."

"How could I know? You don't wear a ring, you came on to me, we had sex! Married men don't do that!"

Steve's look told her she should have known better.

"But I don't do that!" she exclaimed. "I would never have had sex with you—I'd never have gotten involved with you if I'd known! Oh, what have I done?" Lisa sat down and put her face in her hands. She was overwhelmed by guilt and shame. Instead of becoming someone's girlfriend, she had become "the other woman." ∎

Lisa had lived most of her adult life in the very difficult position of wanting to be married and yet wanting to wait for God's provision. Her strong desire for physical intimacy was not being met. Unfortunately her family and friends, while trying to be encouraging, actually hurt her more than they encouraged her. The message they gave her, subtly or not so subtly, was that she would be better off if she were married. They neglected to compliment her courage to live fully regardless of her marital status or her commitment to seek the unique plan God had for her.

Sometimes a woman who wants to be married but has remained single is led to feel that something is wrong with her or that her career must be more important to her than her relationships—that the problem of being single is her fault. Such messages are painful and can be hard to combat. Be aware of how you view being single. The messages we convey begin in our attitudes and thoughts before they are communicated in words. Do you see being in a marital relationship as the ultimate goal in life? How do you view women who are single or who never married? If being married is the ultimate goal, how does a single woman feel about God since he has not provided a husband for her?

In her hunger for a romantic relationship, Lisa avoided asking the obvious questions of the man she was seeing. Sexual intimacy can feel very natural when emotional intimacy is present, even outside of marriage. Lisa allowed her deep desires to lead her to accept the relationship with Steve at face value, without asking the difficult questions about Steve's heart.

For Lisa the issues were far deeper than sexual "freedom." She had believed that if she prayed and was faithful, God would meet her desire for sexual intimacy by providing a marriage partner. How was she to reconcile her understanding that God loved and valued her yet had not provided her with a husband? Certainly her need for emotional intimacy could be met by friends and family, but what about her desire for physical intimacy?

In choosing abstinence, Lisa made choices against the culture. Eventually her naiveté combined with her desire drew her into a relationship with a married man. But what if Steve had not been married? Would it then have been okay to have a physical relationship with him if they were planning to marry? Certainly the culture sends the strong message that two unmarried people in a committed relationship can express their love sexually. But God still plans for the one-flesh union of a man and a woman to take place only within the committed relationship of marriage.

THE INFLUENCE OF FRIENDS

Even very young women—those still in high school and sometimes even younger—may have to fight to follow God's path and maintain sexual integrity. This is not an easy road to walk alone. Friends are essential, but they need to be the right friends, as Beth learned when she moved to a new community a great deal different than her old one.

■ When Beth's parents decided to move during her junior year in high school, Beth's life turned upside down. Not only did her father's job change take the family to a different part of the country, but Beth had to leave the small Christian high school where she had grown up with everyone in her class and enroll in a huge public high school where she knew no one.

Beth now seemed to vacillate between terror and anxiety. At her previous school she had had little interest in the boys; they were all like brothers to her. Besides, everyone in that little town had plans to go to college and probably end up somewhere else. There was little incentive to settle down with a local guy. Beth discovered that the boys here stirred feelings she hadn't felt before.

Coming into this new community was like visiting another planet.

The huge high school had girls who wore black leather, black lipstick, and blue hair; there were jocks who looked like they should be in college and not still stuck in high school; there were nerdy kids who got pushed around by everyone. Beth didn't know where to find a friend. She'd never been tongue-tied talking to anyone; now she found herself self-conscious. Before, she had enjoyed school and been involved in every possible activity; now school was unbearable. She felt she had nothing to offer.

The girls she met at her family's new church offered the most immediate access to potential friends, but her first conversations with them were shocking. Their language was crude. The first word added to her vocabulary was "lustation." In her new circle, the girls seemed to use the term for anything they felt toward a boy beyond noticing he was cute.

RED FLAG: *Do your close friendships discourage your Christian values?* ≡

An evening at the home of one of her new friends deepened her shock. The girls had invited her for pizza and a movie. It turned out to be a film like nothing she had seen before. As the explicit images and sounds of couples having sex filled the room, Beth felt stunned, shocked, and ashamed. She struggled over whether to leave and wondered what that would do for her future with these girls. She admitted to herself that she was also curious. The other girls seemed so casual about this, commenting on the performance as they ate popcorn. She stayed.

After the film, the girls began to talk about their own "adventures." Beth could hardly believe what she was hearing. Descriptions of steamy make-out sessions quickly degenerated into a can-you-top-this contest. Two of the girls debated whether oral sex was really sex.

Then the inevitable happened. One of the girls said, "So Beth, you haven't told us about any of your adventures." Cornered and blushing fiercely, Beth said, "To be honest with you, most of this is new to me. I've always been taught to save sex until marriage."

That brought a chorus of hoots. Beth felt some relief that they seemed to be reacting to her words rather than rejecting her. Another girl finally said, "Beth, you've got a lot to learn. Saving it until marriage? You wouldn't buy a car without test driving it, would you? Can you imagine marrying a man for life you hadn't tried out first? And how can you choose the right car without test driving a lot of them...if you know what I mean?"

When Beth returned home a little later, she lay in bed reliving the entire evening. It was all so foreign to her. Was it all as wrong as it felt? The comments about "test-driving" mocked her commitment to save sex for marriage. And then it struck her. The test-driving image seemed to make sense if she pictured herself as the driver. But what if she turned out to be the car? ■

Beth was vulnerable to the lie that sexual freedom is acceptable because she was thrust into a situation where the lie had taken root. We are far more influenced by our circumstances than we wish to acknowledge. Our school and work environments and our friendships all influence us to hold to certain values. The structures that we place in our lives, including our relationships, can protect and nourish us when we face temptation.

Scripture clearly encourages and commands us to guard our hearts. "Above all else, guard your heart, for it is the wellspring of life" (Proverbs 4:23). Temptation to make poor choices is far harder to resist when our companions are encouraging us to make those poor choices. Beth's new social environment was at odds with her personal views. What a difficult set of options she faced! She could continue to guard her heart and risk being ridiculed and excluded, or she could compromise her beliefs and be accepted by a new group of friends.

RED FLAG: *Are you afraid to speak God's truth into your friends' lives?*

Unfortunately, Beth found that her new friends at church didn't live the values of their faith and wouldn't encourage her to do so. Following Christ doesn't insure that we always will resist temptation, but the encouragement of godly friends to walk a difficult but godly path is invaluable in being able to do so. We were designed to live in relationship and community, and we are responsible for choosing our community. Making wise choices in our friendships can help us resist temptation and provide wise perspectives when we are tempted to act in ways that are not loving or godly.

THE TRUTH

The truth is that God did create us as sexual beings, and He declared that His creation was good! We do have the freedom to express ourselves sexually—within God's plan. We have free will—the ability to choose to follow God or to reject His ways.

In the Garden of Eden, Eve exercised her freedom and chose to disobey God. She gave into the temptation to take matters into her own hands and deliberately ate the fruit that God had commanded Adam and Eve not to eat, and she gave some to Adam who willingly ate it also. The consequences were serious—Adam and Eve received the knowledge of good and evil, and sin and death came into the world. Human nature was no longer what it was meant to be.

We have freedom to choose, but our choices have consequences. The principle applies to all of life, including our relationships. When we take relationships into our own hands apart from God's plan, we also receive the consequences. Take an honest look around you, at yourself and at the women you know. "Don't be misled—you cannot mock the justice of God. You will always harvest what you plant" (Galatians 6:7, NLT).

Our circumstances can be very difficult. It is hard to be married but have the yet-unrealized-hope of experiencing a fulfilling sexual relationship. Some women, like Bonnie, choose to fulfill sexual desires outside their marriages, but there are always consequences. How difficult to long to be married and to continue to wait, as Lisa did, for God's provision of a husband. What a difficult temptation young women like Beth face, having to choose between fitting in or holding to what God says is right.

Whatever our situation, it is tempting to believe that unless we take matters into our own hands, our needs and desires will not be met. We often question God's provision, especially when God's provision means refusing what would be very easy, humanly speaking, to obtain. It can feel right, even logical to do so. We rightly value action and accomplishment, but taking action apart from God's direction and plan is foolish.

The painful difficulty of waiting on God's provision, whatever our situation, is that God doesn't promise us life with sexual fulfillment. That is part of His plan for His children, but not His promise. His promise is far greater—He promises us Himself! John and Stasi Eldredge write in *Captivating*, "He wants intimacy with you in the midst of the madness and the mundane, the meetings and memos, the laundry and lists, the carpools and conversations and projects and pain." Eve doesn't get a do-over, but each of us has many opportunities to choose to love God rather than disobey, to know God and to experience His love. We need to flee temptation, waiting and trusting in God's love for us and His direction for our lives, not our own.

This is not a passive but a very active process! How can waiting be active? When we wait on God, we are fully engaged in relationship—relationship with the true lover of our souls, God Himself! By waiting and by looking to Him for love, care, and direction, we are proclaiming our love for Him with our obedience and our lives. Waiting fixes our eyes on Him in a unique way; we are depending on Him alone. He is the source, and His resources are unlimited. He knows what kind of help we need for our situation, and He will lead us there if we ask Him and are willing to do what He tells us when He answers!

Regardless of our marital status, our first love is none other than the Creator of the universe! God desires our worship and warned His people, the Israelites, of the dangers of idol worship: "You must not have any other God but me. You must not make for yourself an idol of any kind.... You must not bow down to them or worship them" (Deuteronomy 5:7-9, NLT). "Do not worship their gods [those of the Israelites' pagan neighbors], or they will trap you" (Deuteronomy 7:16, NLT). Anything we desire so much that we are willing to disobey God to have it has become our idol—even sexual fulfillment, which God created to be good. The wonderful promise of Scripture to us is this: "Delight yourself in the LORD; and He will give you the desires of your heart" (Psalm 37:4, NASB). God will not ridicule our desires or leave us unsatisfied, but as we delight in Him, He will satisfy us with His love and blessings!

Is sexual freedom good for women? No, a resounding no! *God's* freedom is good for women—and may or may not include sexual satisfaction, but it will certainly include a rich joy and delight in Him! "Taste and see that the LORD is good" (Psalm 34:8). If God has provided you with a marriage partner, then a fulfilling sexual relationship is potentially yours to enjoy. But regardless of your marital status or the condition of your marriage, God wants to be the lover of your soul and will provide enjoyment and joy!

take action

✓ Does God delight in you as a woman? If you cannot answer a swift yes to this question, ask God to reveal to you what is coming between you and His delight.

✓ Do you have at least two friends who support your values, your relationship with Jesus, and your marriage or your singleness? If not, are you willing to find a group of women in your church or a church in your community that holds those values?

✓ Take some time to pray about your view of singleness. Learn how God views singleness.

✓ Find and begin a good Bible reading plan. Ask your husband or a friend to join you on the adventure of discovering God through His Word.

✓ How do you "delight yourself in the Lord"? Do you enjoy spending time with Him? Do you pull away from the busyness of the world and seek Him, as you would a lover? Here is a way to begin—find a special place and go there alone with a notebook and a Bible and a cup of coffee or tea, if you wish. Ask the Lord to be with you and to speak to you there!

✓ Rejoice in the Lord's love for you. Finding wonderful music to sing and dance to can be a way to bring you into his presence!

✓ If sexual temptation is a problem, find a trusted friend to talk to about this, someone who will pray with and for you.

Lie #3

Sexual temptation will go away once I'm married.

Stacey's downcast eyes reflect the lingering pain of events that took place more than two years ago. After a few halting starts, she finally says simply, "Two years ago I admitted to my husband, Bob, that I'd been unfaithful to him.

"For weeks I agonized about telling him the truth. The affair—a terrible, terrible mistake—was over. I kept thinking, why did he need to know? At first, I decided that keeping it secret was best, but then I wondered if my motivation was to spare Bob the pain or me the shame.

"In the end, I had no choice: My emotions were a jumble of contradictions and wouldn't stay under wraps. Bob didn't believe me when I blamed my mood swings on PMS or my inability to return his hugs on my preoccupation with work. I was constantly emotional, and the guilt I felt inside kept showing up in my outward actions. I either neglected Bob completely, turning away from his affections, or I tried too hard and ran myself ragged with perfectionism. Bob couldn't help but notice my strange behavior, and I had run out of lies."

Stacey looks away, shifts in her chair, and then starts again.

"I was forty-one when it began, and I thought what every good Christian woman thinks—that I was an unlikely candidate for an extramarital affair. Bob and I had been married for nineteen years and were active in our church. I'd just taken a job as a secretary in a large public relations firm in the hope of boosting our kids' college fund. Most of my friends already had found their way back to careers they'd put on hold when they married. For a long time I had envied their shop talk, expanding responsibilities, updated wardrobes, and the occasional splurges their salaries allowed. I thought it was finally my turn to have those things. But I had no intention of looking for anything more than that. When something more came looking for me, I wasn't prepared.

"Three days into my new job, I had my doubts about my new career venture. I felt overwhelmed and old. My skills were rusty, and my confidence level was nonexistent. After a couple of minutes in front of a computer screen, I wanted to wave a white flag and go home.

"My supervisor quickly assigned Dave, the resident technology whiz, to bail me out. His duties included training new employees on the office information system. He later joked that I was his greatest challenge. He recognized my insecurity and said all the right words of encouragement. He teased me just enough to help me relax and then proposed a crash course in data retrieval—whatever that was.

"And here's where I should have drawn the line, but I didn't: He was also willing to schedule a couple of Saturday morning sessions—which meant being in the office alone together—and reward my progress with follow-up lunches. He sent me funny messages via e-mail and insisted I respond so I could learn the right codes and commands. Instead of resisting, I eagerly participated in this silent dialogue and didn't stop several weeks later when his notes took on a decidedly personal tone.

"Dave seemed to notice everything about me—a change in hairstyle, a different perfume—and wasted no time in complimenting me. Although his attention set off internal warning signals, I ignored them. After all, I figured, I'm an adult, I'm a Christian, and I'm married. I thought I could halt our friendship anytime it became uncomfortable.

"You're probably wondering why I so readily accepted all this attention from Dave, and I have asked myself that a hundred times. On the surface, my marriage seemed strong enough to withstand any threat. For years Bob and I had enjoyed a warm, comfortable relationship, maybe short on spontaneity but long on commitment. I loved Bob and he loved me, and daily assurances came not in words but in our willingness to pitch in and share responsibilities.

RED FLAG: *Is there a relationship your husband thinks is safe but there are secrets about the relationship that you are not telling him?*

"I never thought about the absence of romance in our marriage until it suddenly reappeared in my life—courtesy of Dave—in the form of silly cards propped against my coffee mug, flowers tucked under my windshield wipers, and little notes tacked to my computer screen. I was being pursued—and it felt good.

"I found myself comparing Bob to Dave and always giving Dave the edge. Bob was dependable, Dave was exciting; Bob made me feel secure, Dave made me feel young; Bob wanted to build a future, Dave wanted to enjoy the present.

"I didn't want to talk to anyone about my confusion, because then I'd have to justify my growing attachment to a man who wasn't my husband. I gradually withdrew from my family, our church, and our friends. They only reminded me that what I was doing was wrong.

RED FLAG: *Have you begun to frequently compare your husband to someone else you have a relationship with?* ≣

"My new job with its long hours provided the perfect excuse for my spotty attendance at Wednesday night Bible study and for my decision to drop out of our church's couples class. Bob and our daughters never questioned my need to spend evenings in the den with stacks of papers from the office."

Stacey pauses, gazing into her empty mug, and, after a heavy sigh, continues.

"My involvement with Dave progressed from professional to emotional to sexual. I hated my double life and the lies I told to support it. Three months later, when my guilt became unbearable, I requested a transfer to a suburban office, a move that put Dave physically, if not emotionally, out of my life. I missed him, but I didn't miss the deception that was the foundation of the relationship. He accepted my decision with little argument, causing me to believe our affair meant much more to me than to him. This realization only added to my agony over what I had done.

"Distance brought clarity—and with it, more guilt. I tried to pretend the affair never happened, but it had—and my conscience wouldn't let me forget. I tried to get back in touch with my family and church, but those contacts made my secret more unbearable.

"I couldn't understand why I couldn't just put the whole thing behind me. I hadn't been caught and I was even being held up as a role model—the working wife and mom who successfully juggled career and family. But every time a friend said, 'I wish I were more like you,' I wanted to scream. I didn't deserve admiration.

RED FLAG: *Do you find yourself withdrawing from your friends because of what is happening in your life?* ≣

"My need to confess eventually led to telling Bob the truth. He had suspected something was wrong. I felt emotionally numb and had difficulty responding to his need for intimacy.

"His love and trust were daily reminders of my unworthiness. I had to pay for my actions, and, since he was the victim, I wanted him to deal me a harsh punishment. Still, I dreaded the confrontation and imagined what the range of his reactions would be: disbelief, then hurt, then anger.

"I never expected the response I got when I finally told him. After the tears, after the angry questions, he said that we had to save our marriage and that we had to try to forgive each other. He had to forgive me for my infidelity; I had to forgive him for whatever had been lacking in our marriage that had made me vulnerable.

"I was shocked. I hadn't expected any talk of forgiveness. I almost wanted him to leave me or hit me or do something drastic that I deserved. Not try to forgive me.

"We knew it would be a long road. We weren't sure we could do it. But after much talk and many tears, we knew that with God's help we wanted to try. And that as hard as it would be for Bob to forgive me, it would be even harder for me to forgive myself."

Stacey's eyes fill with tears and her voice wavers as she continues. "Healing has come slowly, and we are still not completely there. More than a year passed before I'd sufficiently forgiven myself so I could accept God's grace. Up to that point, my faith seemed to increase my guilt instead of ease it. Familiar verses about fidelity and commitment jumped off the pages of my Bible, haunting instead of helping me. They reminded me that as a Christian, I'd known the difference between right and wrong, yet I'd sinned anyway. Ignorance was no excuse for my actions. The burden of being a believer never seemed heavier.

"Our marriage was fragile, so Bob and I looked for ways to strengthen it. We tried too hard to make up for our mistakes. I overcompensated by acting the part of the perfect wife and mother, fussing with meals, keeping a spotless house, doting on our daughters. Bob struggled to be more demonstrative by bringing me flowers and calling me from work just to say hello. Privately, I wondered if he was checking to see if I was at home when I said I would be. Could he ever trust me again?

"We read a how-to book about revitalizing relationships and laughed at our clumsiness in carrying out its advice." Stacey smiles though her eyes fill with tears. "The laughter did more good than the advice, and we decided there was a lesson in that too. We needed to laugh and talk more.

"We attended a marriage enrichment seminar and picked through the platitudes for something that might ease our hurt. We visited a Christian counselor who helped us understand that 'comfortable' marriages aren't always healthy ones. Prayer together became an essential part of our daily life and recovery.

"Two years after my affair, our life is beginning to come together. Although I still don't fully understand what caused me to do what I did, I know now that Christians, like everyone else, are vulnerable to temptation. And I understand that a marriage, even a good one, requires constant nurturing to sustain it.

"Our relationship will never be the same, because we will never be the same. Trust has eroded, but perhaps in time it will be replenished. The fact that my unfaithfulness didn't become common knowledge now seems like a gift from God. He gave me a second chance, and I pray I'll know what to do with it." ■

Stacey's assumption that her marriage would protect her from an affair was erroneous. Marriage, even a good one, is not protection enough from such temptation, and nowhere does the Bible tell us that it will be. In fact, just the opposite is true. Why else would the Bible say, "Marriage should be honored by all, and the marriage bed kept pure" (Hebrews 13:4)?

As women in today's world, we have opportunities to live and move outside the circles of our homes and families that were unknown just a few generations ago. And our culture increasingly relies on sex to solve every problem and meet every need. We really do need to be on our guard, as the writer of the book of Proverbs tells us: "Above all else, guard your heart" (Proverbs 4:23).

DECEPTION AND PROTECTION

Friendships with men other than your husband can easily cross the line. If you're not on your guard, sometimes you may not even know that you are headed for the line, let alone almost across it. So how do you evaluate friendships with other men?

First, don't deceive yourself. Sin often carries with it a blindness to the truth. One of the lies associated with sin is that we are in control and can change our behavior anytime we want to. You may find yourself saying that you can end a relationship whenever you want to, but in reality you are deceiving yourself. Your relationship, like an addiction, has already gotten a grip on your life.

Also important to remember is that if you have any relationship with a secret component, you are already in trouble. Marriages are relationships of oneness, and keeping secrets from your husband tears at that unity.

One of our most valuable gifts in these situations is our conscience and that innate set of warning bells that tell us we are moving into danger. When our conscience is tuned in to God's ways, it is an effective warning system. Ignoring or trying to disconnect our warning system leaves us vulnerable to sin.

Telling ourselves lies can numb our consciences. If you are telling yourself, "I can stop this relationship anytime I want to" or "This relationship isn't really wrong because it's just a friendship," you are deceiving yourself. In effect, you are turning off your conscience. And one of the most deceptive lies is: "This isn't really wrong because it isn't a sexual relationship." If you are thinking like this, then the friendship you are evaluating is *not* good for your marriage.

Resolving not to deceive yourself is one of the best things you can do to keep your friendships within safe boundaries. A second protection against temptation is having close relationships with friends who support us in our faith. When we allow our friends to know our struggles and temptations, when we can feel their support, when we know they are praying for us, we are stronger.

Giving your friends permission to ask you about your relationships helps you make wise choices. When you know you have to face friends who will ask about your day or week, you can find strength to resist temptation. On the other hand, if you find yourself closing others out or moving away from the accountability of friendships, that is likely a huge warning sign that you are engaged in behaviors that will harm your marriage.

Putting physical distance or separation between you and the other person can be an effective way to bring an end to a relationship. But distance itself is not always enough to allow you to move on. You may feel that because you have ended a wrong relationship, you should be able to pick up your normal life again and move on. But that won't work if other unresolved issues hold you back from finding the help and healing you need.

HELP AND HEALING

One of the biggest issues that prevents us from healing our lives is refusing to forgive ourselves. When we won't or can't forgive ourselves, we remain trapped in the past, making us vulnerable to further temptation and sin. Sometimes we feel worthless and want to punish ourselves; sometimes we believe that God could not possibly forgive the magnitude of our sins. Such feelings and misguided beliefs can underlie our refusal to accept God's forgiveness.

But God's grace to us is undeserved. When we confess our sins and turn from them, we *are* forgiven. Accepting God's forgiveness allows us to reaffirm our faith in Him and in His care for us.

Sometimes, though, we need to experience acceptance and forgiveness from others in order to be able to accept God's forgiveness. That's another reason friends and others we trust are so important in our lives. Not only can they help us withstand temptation, they can become part of our healing process also. When others know us as we really are and still accept and forgive us, we grow, our hearts become secure, and we can accept God's forgiveness and move on.

■ Stacey refused to listen to the warning signals she was given. She knew that her "friendship" with Dave was crossing the line, but she told herself that she could end the relationship anytime she wished. Her determination to keep the relationship secret was another warning signal she ignored.

When Stacey could no longer stand the guilt her behavior was causing, she ended the relationship by changing jobs. She believed that if she ended the relationship, she would be able to move on, but her unresolved guilt over betraying her husband kept her from being able to go on as if nothing had happened. Fortunately, when she confessed her sin to her husband, his desire was to forgive her and to move forward with the marriage. But even if Bob had not been willing to forgive his wife, bringing the affair into the light rather than keeping it hidden in the darkness was the right thing for Stacey to do. Since she was having trouble forgiving herself for the affair, it was essential that she experience forgiveness from another so she could accept God's forgiveness, forgive herself, and move on.

Stacey's story has a difficult but hopeful new beginning forged from the pain of her poor choices. She now knows the depth of her husband's love and his willingness to commit to her, but she also knows the ongoing pain of trust that has been depleted. Trust is built over time but can be destroyed very quickly. The process of rebuilding trust is like building a brick wall, one trustworthy act at a time. After an affair, the process is neither fast nor easy, but Stacey's husband is willing to be part of the process, to be a partner in the rebuilding.

DREAMS AND DESIRE

One way of understanding affairs is that they are energy moved from the marriage into another relationship, as Blanca discovered when she enrolled in college as a newlywed.

■ Blanca met Arturo in high school in Chicago. He was a forward on the soccer team, and she was a big fan who never missed a game, especially when she started dating Arturo during their junior year. High school was a whirlwind of activity, and Blanca and Arturo looked forward to life together. Arturo wanted to become a state trooper; Blanca thought all she wanted was to be married to Arturo and to have children. They talked about these plans during their favorite "cheap date"—going to Grant Park, watching Buckingham Fountain, and then wandering the walking paths along the Lake Michigan lakefront. They became engaged senior year and married soon after graduation.

While Arturo trained to become a state trooper, Blanca took care of their small apartment and visited with friends. The couple still enjoyed their walks on the lakefront, but when until Arturo was hired as a bilingual trooper in the southern suburbs, Blanca and Arturo needed to relocate. For the first few weeks, Blanca enjoyed "nesting"—setting up their tiny apartment and just being a wife. She collected recipes and worked hard to have special meals on the table when Arturo got home.

RED FLAG: *Are your dreams and the pursuit of those dreams taking you away from your husband or separating you from him?* ≡

Blanca hoped she could get pregnant right away, but as the months slid by and nothing happened, she decided that working would help pay the bills and also give her something to do. Being bilingual in English and Spanish helped her land a job at the local community college as an administrative assistant. Arturo was put on the night shift, and dinners together became a thing of the past.

As more months passed, Blanca became more discouraged because she was not getting pregnant. She and Arturo barely crossed paths because of the differences in their work hours, but still they tried to have times of intimacy. They scheduled time together, and Blanca worked hard to make sure they were intimate at times that would allow them the highest possibility of getting pregnant. But nothing worked.

Blanca's supervisor saw in her a hardworking and dedicated employee, and he wanted to see Blanca work on classes toward an associate's degree. He suggested that Blanca take some business classes at the college.

"Guess what?" Blanca told Arturo that weekend. "My supervisor wants me to take some classes. Business classes. I can get an associate's degree. Arturo, I never thought I'd do anything like that! What do you think?"

"Wow, that would be great for you," Arturo said. "I know we're really working on the pregnancy thing, but maybe this is the time for you to get a degree. I say go for it. You always liked being a student and learning new things. As long as you feel like it won't be too much for you, I'm behind you one hundred ten percent."

Arturo was right; Blanca had been a good student in high school, and some of her teachers had encouraged her to go on to college, but it had never been in her plan. Now she sensed that this might be the perfect opportunity for her to continue her studies in an area that interested her.

That's how Blanca landed in an evening class on business ethics seated next to Kirk. Blanca and Kirk chatted the first evening and hit it off quickly. The next week the friendship made it easy to walk together to the coffee machine during their break and to decide to work together on a class project.

With Arturo working the night shift, Blanca was willing to stay late after class to work with Kirk as needed; that was easier than getting together another night during the week. She and Kirk began to make it a habit to go to a nearby restaurant, order dessert and coffee, and spread out their books on the table.

They enjoyed talking. Kirk was currently in business for himself— trying to run a small T-shirt printing business. Blanca was fascinated with the ins and outs of running a business, the government regulations, the accounting, the forms, the taxes, the issues with employees. She was learning so much from Kirk.

She talked with Arturo about the classes and casually mentioned Kirk and his business. She enjoyed telling Arturo about all that she was learning about owning a small business. They began to consider what it would take for Blanca to start her own party-planning business. They both knew that Blanca could do amazing things with the simplest get-together. Arturo was thrilled with all that Blanca was thinking about and glad to see his wife so excited.

Blanca began to share some of these dreams with Kirk. He had lots of input: questions she should ask, things she should think about, how to get her ducks in the proverbial row before taking the leap. Blanca was excited to see her own horizons opening up. Imagine actually making money doing something that she loved!

RED FLAG: *When you receive good news at work or at school, is there someone you want to tell before you tell your husband?* ≋

Blanca and Kirk continued to work on their class project one night a week at the restaurant. Separately, Kirk worked on T-shirts to give to the other class members as part of their presentation, while Blanca prepared handouts. When the day came for them to do their presentation, their enthusiasm for what they were learning clearly showed through. Kirk and Blanca batted their topic back and forth, spoke with confidence, and even joked at the right moments. The teacher was impressed, and so were the other students.

On the way out the door, one of the female students casually observed to Blanca, "You guys seem to be in love with this class and each other!"

Blanca was too shocked to respond. What had she done? She

hadn't really stopped to think about what she felt for Kirk. She loved being with him. He was fun; he helped her with her dreams; he helped her with the class. But was she in love with him? No, she loved Arturo. Still, she had to admit that she wasn't this enthusiastic with or about her wonderful husband. How had she let her feelings for a man other than Arturo get so out of control? ■

Few activities are more energy producing than dreams becoming reality! Engaging in new experiences and discovering new ideas can be very exciting and often serve to enrich a marriage. Growth in our lives can translate into growth in our relationships.

Blanca's energy and excitement for her classes translated into dreams for her own life. But rather than allowing the energy to flow from her own life into the marriage, Blanca formed a relationship with a man who was not her husband, and the energy flowed between *them* instead.

Although Arturo was supportive of Blanca's new endeavors, Blanca began to share her dreams with Kirk more than with Arturo. The connection between Blanca and Kirk grew out of their shared interests, and Blanca wasn't even aware that she was putting her marriage in jeopardy.

The comment of a fellow student served as a well-timed wake-up call for Blanca. Sometimes the beginnings of an attraction develop in a hidden way, apart from our awareness, underneath the excitement of learning new things or working on a project together. Even working together in a church ministry creates opportunities to transfer the excitement and satisfaction of serving to a relationship with someone you are serving with. Fortunately, Blanca received some helpful feedback about the nature of her relationship with Kirk, and she took it to heart.

What drew Blanca and Arturo to each other while they were dating was time spent together. But then their schedules changed—Arturo began working the night shift and Blanca went back to school—and much of the casual time they had spent together diminished. They may not have noticed their lack of time together, but it was a factor that made it easier for Blanca to spend time with Kirk.

"I DO"

It can be very difficult to honor our marriage commitments if we haven't thought seriously about what we are doing when we agree to marry, as Sandy discovered just two weeks after her wedding.

■ Sandy started crying again. Every time she thought about her situation, tears flowed.

She had met Pete during their senior year of college and experienced a whirlwind romance. After college, Sandy got an apartment, and Pete soon moved in with her. Their jobs kept them busy, and sharing an apartment and all the expenses that went with it just made sense—and of course there were "fringe benefits," too.

Sandy's parents were not happy about this arrangement. That didn't matter much to Sandy, but after a while the pressure became more intense. Pete didn't want to make enemies of Sandy's parents, and he suggested that maybe they should make their relationship legal. Sandy finally capitulated, figuring that setting a wedding date would calm the waters with her family. Besides, a wedding meant a vacation!

Pete and Sandy weren't into wedding planning (and Sandy's mom was happy to oblige), but they focused on planning a terrific honeymoon trip. Searching the Internet and checking out vacation deals, they planned a getaway trip to an exotic island where they could bask in the sun, play in the waves, and maybe try some exotic food. That almost made it bearable to deal with a wedding!

Then came the envelope from Uncle Sam. Pete was in the Army Reserves, and now he was being notified that he was being sent overseas for a year. His departure date was two weeks after their wedding. Suddenly, Sandy's mental pictures of a romantic honeymoon were overshadowed by a huge dark cloud of uncertainty. Apart for a year right after the wedding? How would that work?

Sandy's mind was in a whirl. Why should they even get married? Why tie herself down? If something happened to Pete, she'd rather not be a widow... she'd want to be able just to go on with her life. She felt terrible about having such thoughts. She didn't want to tell Pete what she was thinking. She was angry that Pete had to leave, angry about the timing, angry about the uncertainty. But the wedding was looming, the invitations sent. They'd come too far to turn back now, hadn't they?

For Pete and Sandy, the wedding day had an echo of sadness; the cloud of uncertainty remained on the horizon. Instead of relaxing on their honeymoon, they both felt despair and dread; they were irritable and on edge. Previous intimacy made the sexual part of the honeymoon something familiar and almost disappointing. When they finally returned to their apartment, both were already wondering if they had made a mistake.

The next week presented a myriad of details to be finalized before Pete left. When they finally said good-bye at the airport, it seemed that they'd had no time at all to feel really married.

RED FLAG: *How do you and your husband handle separations?* ≡

About a month after Pete was deployed, Sandy came home from work and noticed the answering machine light flashing. When she pressed the button, she heard a familiar voice; it was Joel, a boyfriend from college. "I'm in town for a week, and I decided to look you up and was surprised to find you listed in the phone book," the message began. "I thought for sure you'd be married by now!" The phone was still in Sandy's name.

Joel had been a fun boyfriend—and he had been Sandy's first sexual experience. Her memories of that first time were vivid. These thoughts coursed through her mind as the message ended with "I was wondering, would you like to have dinner with me?"

It's innocent enough, she thought. Just dinner with an old friend. It might be fun to think about old times and get away from the sadness I've been feeling.

But you're married now, prodded a little voice in her head.

The problem was, Sandy just didn't feel married. She played the message again, her finger poised over the erase button. But the desire for companionship, for an old friend, for something to ease the pain overwhelmed her. Instead of pressing erase, she reached for a pen and wrote down the phone number. She knew she crossed a line when she did that. She didn't know how far she would go. ■

Living together is very different than being married. Sandy and Pete might have felt like they knew each other and that after the wedding there would be no surprises, but in reality the finality of a marriage commitment changes a relationship. While Sandy and Pete had plenty of time to get used to what it was like to live together, they had little time to work on being married. A separation so soon after the wedding put them both at risk.

In addition, with Pete so far away, Sandy was especially vulnerable. How would they both work to keep their love alive and strengthen their relationship when the distance made communication difficult? Sandy had no support system in place to help her cope with a long-distance relationship.

An even deeper problem in their relationship was that they both felt ambivalent about getting married in the first place. They based their decision to get married on pleasing Sandy's parents and the excitement of a honeymoon; their desire to commit to one another came in a low third place. Sandy and Pete drifted into marriage without a clear understanding of why they were choosing each other to be partners for life. They were not able to talk through these issues before Pete was deployed and they had to begin a long separation.

As with Stacey in the first story in this chapter, Sandy's conscience set off warning bells—before the wedding when Sandy realized she was uneasy about the wedding and afterward when she received the phone message from Joel. Both times she knew what course of action she *should* take, but rather than do the difficult right thing she chose to take the easier wrong action.

By writing down Joel's phone number, Sandy took the first step toward renewing an old relationship. In her current emotional state, the temptation provided in seeing Joel again would be very difficult to resist. Sandy knew this, but she didn't have a plan for resisting the temptation or for dealing with her loneliness and confusion. Support groups for military spouses, proactive ways to cope with loneliness, friends to confide in, and even a counselor to help sort through the confusion—all should have been in place to help her deal with her husband's absence.

THE TRUTH

The statement that sexual temptation will go away after marriage is a lie. We are created for relationship. Whenever we choose to connect emotionally with someone other than our husbands, the possibility of sexual temptation exists.

The truth is that even a good marriage does not protect against sexual temptation. We all can be tempted to choose wrong ways to fulfill our desires, even when our desires are for the right things. Remember that "the temptations in your life are no different from what others experience" (1 Corinthians 10:13, NLT). The good news is that we do not have to battle our temptations alone, and there *is* a way out.

The battle against sexual temptation in our lives is essentially a spiritual one. The Bible identifies Satan as our enemy; his goal is to destroy us. The apostle Peter wrote, "Be self-controlled and alert. Your enemy the devil prowls around like a roaring lion looking for someone to devour" (1 Peter 5:8).

Satan is the source of our temptations, and he uses what he finds in our own hearts. If there is any weakness in our marriage relationship at all, Satan will use it against us. James wrote, "Each one is tempted when, by his own evil desire, he is dragged away and enticed. Then, after desire has conceived, it gives birth to sin" (James 1:14–15).

We need God's spiritual armor to fight a spiritual war; God provides protection and provision for us through His Word and His Spirit:

A final word: Be strong with the Lord and in his mighty power. Put on all of God's armor so that you will be able to stand firm against all strategies of the devil. For we are not fighting against flesh-and-blood enemies, but against evil rulers and authorities of the unseen world, against mighty powers in this dark world, and against evil spirits in the heavenly places.

Therefore, put on every piece of God's armor so you will be able to resist the enemy in the time of evil Then after the battle you will still be standing firm. Stand your ground, putting on the belt of truth and the body armor of God's righteousness. For shoes, put on the peace that comes from the Good News, so that you will be fully prepared. In addition to all of these, hold up the shield of faith to stop the fiery arrows of the devil. Put on salvation as your helmet, and take the sword of the Spirit, which is the word of God.

Pray in the Spirit at all times and on every occasion. Stay alert and be persistent in your prayers for all believers everywhere. (Ephesians 6:10-18, NLT)

The Bible reminds us that we need to draw on God's strength when we are tempted and not try to resist temptation by ourselves. God has promised us a way out of temptation: "And God is faithful. He will not allow the temptation to be more than you can stand. When you are tempted, he will show you a way out so that you can endure" (1 Corinthians 10:13, NLT). With God, our weaknesses become our strengths when we acknowledge our dependence on Him and rely on Him. Paul wrote, "That is why, for Christ's sake, I delight in weaknesses, in insults, in hardships, in persecutions, in difficulties. For when I am weak, then I am strong" (2 Corinthians 12:10).

One way God provides help to us is through other trusted

believers. Admitting our temptations to trustworthy people is one way to "speak the truth in love" (see Ephesians 4:15). Sometimes, as Dr. Henry Cloud writes about in *How People Grow,* we need help and resources from outside ourselves until we have developed the inner strength we need. Friends can pray for us, be available to talk when we are facing temptation, and regularly ask us how we are handling tempting situations. "A person standing alone can be attacked and defeated, but two can stand back-to-back and conquer. Three are even better, for a triple-braided cord is not easily broken" (Ecclesiastes 4:12, NLT).

take action

✓ Be proactive about keeping the energy in your marriage!
What do you and your husband enjoy doing together?
Continue to develop shared interests and dreams.

✓ Being involved together in a service project or ministry
in the church is an excellent way to share together.

✓ When you feel attracted to someone who is not your husband,
think about why the attraction is occurring. Is there something
in your marriage relationship that is making you vulnerable?
Examine your marriage and take steps to improve it.

✓ What in your relationship with this other person
is creating temptation for you? Take steps to create
appropriate safeguards to prevent you from spending one-
on-one time with the person you are attracted to.

✓ Enlist a close friend to confide in when you are faced
with sexual temptation, and ask her to pray for you.

✓ If you see a friend involved in a close relationship with a man
other than her husband and warning bells are going off in you,
find a way to speak with her about it. Don't assume she is aware
of the danger.

Lie #4

My husband doesn't understand me. I deserve someone who does.

Susan and Philip have been married for four years. They live in an apartment near the university campus where Susan is an assistant professor of music. When they met in college, the old saying "opposites attract" described them perfectly, and it still does. They could not be more different.

Philip is a jock—he loves participating in and watching sports. In college he was "big man on campus" and first string on the football team. Now he works as a bank manager, but in his free time he's always at the gym or outside on his bicycle. Philip eats right, exercises, and stays in great shape. Susan loves her music. She spends most of her time inside, giving private lessons, listening to music, and preparing lesson plans.

In college, Susan's sensitivity to the beauty in music made Philip feel like he was finding another world outside the sports arena. Susan took him to concerts and operas and, while it was difficult at first, he began to see what it might be like to actually appreciate music. And he got to be with Susan on these excursions, which was all that really mattered. Susan, for her part, tried to step into Philip's world as well. She even began to master the rules of football! She loved that Philip was in such great shape—a real hunk of a man. Not a bad catch for this little music major!

They were married in a ceremony laden with beautiful works of music. The wedding day was perfect, and they were perfectly happy as they settled into their jobs and daily lives.

That's when life began to get difficult.

"You need to start working out more," Philip said one Saturday morning as he drank his health shake. "You're getting a little flabby there," he laughed, patting her rear end. He meant it as a joke—sort of. He was serious about the working out part. "I could put together a workout program for you."

"Oh, Phil, I just don't have time for that. With lessons and recitals and class planning, when would I get to the gym?"

"Go in early, like I do," he suggested. "The gym opens at five."

"Right. You know I'm up until at least midnight grading papers."

"Well, you ought to do something. You need to stay healthy and tone up a bit." With that, he put his empty glass in the sink and left.

Susan went upstairs to shower, took off her robe, and looked at herself in the mirror. "My body's not perfect, but it's not terrible," she muttered. "I'll worry about getting to the gym when I have more time."

Their schedules began to differ as well as their priorities. Philip was at work or working out; Susan was at school or giving lessons or grading papers. She went to bed late; he got up early.

Philip's comments became more cutting. Maybe he just wanted her to be healthy, but it seemed to Susan that all he cared about was that she have a body like the women in all those fitness magazines he read. It wasn't going to happen. Susan found solace in her office. She began working there to grade her papers and do her lesson plans, not wanting to come home and face Philip's assault on her flabby arms and thighs.

Philip stopped in one day, with flowers. "Oh, Philip, how nice," Susan said with delight. But inside the envelope was a membership card to the local gym. "Philip, we've talked about this. It won't be worth the money for the membership. I don't have time to go! Why does this matter so much to you?"

Philip exploded. He tried to keep his voice down, but his words came out in loud, harsh whispers. "If you don't do something, we won't be having sex anymore. I just don't find you attractive." Then he stormed out.

Susan looked at the flowers and the card through tears. "He just doesn't understand that this isn't important to me," she whispered to herself. "I look okay. What's the big deal?" She could hardly believe that this was causing so much tension in their relationship.

There was a knock on her office door. It was Matt, the new graduate assistant. He was tall, handsome, and talented. Susan had met him at orientation a few weeks before. "Hi, Susan," he began. "I don't mean to intrude, but... these walls are kind of thin, and I was concerned..."

"I'm fine," Susan said. "You're very kind. That was my husband, Philip. He's under a lot of stress at work. 'Sticks and stones' and all that. I'm sorry we disturbed you."

Matt smiled. "That's okay. Sticks and stones, huh? Not to be rude, but it sounded to me like those were pretty painful sticks and stones. I've always thought 'but names will never hurt me' is about the biggest lie around."

"Yes, well, I guess I've got to agree with you there." She put the gym membership card into her purse.

"Nice flowers." Matt was in no hurry to leave. Susan was feeling self-conscious. They both stood staring at the flowers.

"How about lunch later?" Matt asked. "Want to join me?"

Why not? My husband certainly won't care! Susan thought bitterly. "That would be nice, Matt," she said. "I'd like to get to know you better, since you're working right next door." She tried to make it sound innocent, but her insides were trembling.

Over lunch they talked about music and opera and the latest teaching methods. Matt asked Susan's advice on how to teach a couple of his courses. They laughed. They connected. Matt found Susan amazing in every way—he thought she was a wonderful teacher. Susan found Matt to be a sensitive and wonderful listener, appreciative of her qualities, and amazing in his own right.

Susan continued to keep longer hours at work, and Matt often joined her in her office, working alongside her or discussing some problem with a class or a student. Every day he said something sweet and kind, making her feel like a queen. He didn't seem to mind that she wasn't in great shape; in fact, he seemed to appreciate the shape she had! She found herself dressing in tighter sweaters and wearing a bit more makeup.

RED FLAG: *Do you dress differently if you know you will be seeing a certain man?* ≡

Philip noticed one day. "You really shouldn't wear that sweater. It's too tight on you. It shows your fat."

That same evening, Susan and Matt were working side by side at the piano, discussing some accompanying techniques. The closeness seemed more than she could bear; she put her hand on his and looked into his eyes. The next thing she knew, he had put his arm around her waist and she moved in closer to him. She knew it was wrong, but it felt too good to stop.

Besides, Matt understood her in a way that Philip never would. ■

In her book, *The Monogamy Myth*, about surviving affairs, Peggy Vaughan conducted a survey in which participants were asked if their partner had an affair, what would be the most difficult to overcome—that the person had sex with someone else or that the person deceived them? The results were surprising: 72 percent of the women and 70 percent of the men answered that the deception would be harder to overcome. Only 28 percent of the women and 30 percent of the men answered that it would be more difficult to overcome the fact that their partner had sex with someone else. Sometimes people rationalize that if a relationship does not include sex, it can't be an affair. But an "emotional affair," an extramarital relationship that has not yet become sexual, can still be extremely damaging to a marriage.

Like all dangerous lies, the lie that "if my husband doesn't understand me, I deserve someone who does" contains an element of truth. We all desire to be known and understood. It may be true that your husband doesn't understand you. It may be true that you and he have grown in very different directions. What is *not* true is that the answer is to find someone new. It seems to make sense, but it's a lie.

First of all, it's a lie because it ignores the true root of the problem. Philip and Susan have very different interests, and *those different interests attracted them to each other when they were dating*. In other words, the differences were a plus before they were married but became a problem after. What changed? Philip began to demand that Susan do what he wanted, and Susan became defensive and shut him out. They stopped trying to stay connected to each other's worlds and trying voluntarily to understand each other.

When you were dating, you were eager for your future husband to know how interested you were in every thought he had. You tried to join in his interests; you cared about what he cared about. And, chances are, he did the same for you. However, years have passed. After marriage, more time together is spent doing chores and the day-to-day work of living. Your talk time gets taken up by work and kids—and when you *do* get a chance to talk, you discuss money and bills and house and children. Less and less time is spent actually continuing to get to know each other. That's the root of the problem. The lie says you need to find someone new; the truth is that you need to reconnect with the husband you have.

"If my husband doesn't understand me, I deserve someone who does" also is a lie because it implies that you are *entitled* to find someone new if your husband is not meeting your needs. That twists the words of Scripture that call us to "serve one another in love" (Galatians 5:13), making what *you* want of paramount importance.

You've lived together, slept together, seen each other at your very best—and at your very worst. The familiarity of marriage sets in. If you both haven't been careful to continue to get to know each other, you'll think that there's nothing new to this man, nothing will ever change, and he's just not doing it for you anymore. If you begin to focus on yourself, you'll worry simply about your own survival and your personal happiness. Then you'll be ripe for the lie that you deserve someone else—someone better.

The marriage covenant is meant to last forever—that's a long time. Time enough for there to be pain and difficulty. Time enough for there to be change. But the biblical directive doesn't change. We are to love our husbands even if our own needs are not being met. Admittedly, this isn't easy.

WHAT WOMEN WANT

The "if my husband doesn't understand me, I deserve someone who does" lie does *not* negate the fact that we have been created with a strong desire to be known and understood. If those who are closest to us don't understand and appreciate us (for whatever reason), then we feel the loss as a deep wound. Especially in marriage, women expect and deeply desire to be known and loved. After all, the biblical expression for physical intimacy in the Old Testament is "to know." The King James Version says, "And Adam *knew* Eve his wife; and she conceived, and bare Cain" (Genesis 4:1, italics added). When we marry and commit to sharing our physical bodies with a man, we hope that will be an expression of our husband's deep understanding of who we are.

Understanding our interests and opinions is not enough, however; we wives also need our husbands to understand our *feelings*. When you share with your husband your distress over a situation at work or with a friend, what response do you receive? It may very well be that your husband (being the man that he is) wants to jump in and protect you, or he may give you all kinds of advice for how to solve your dilemma, or he may just turn back to the TV and not appear to have heard you at all (perhaps because he just doesn't know how to help). Many men don't understand that simple statements such as "That must be frustrating for you" or "I bet you felt sad when that happened" go a long way toward helping you feel heard and understood.

WORK TOWARD UNDERSTANDING

Communication in a relationship as important as marriage is hard work! You may think that this process of being known happens automatically simply because you're occupying the same living space with your husband. You may also hope that your husband will understand you in ways that you aren't even able to understand yourself. Disillusionment sets in when we have casual friendships with other men who seem to understand us in ways that our husbands, who live with us and are committed to us, can't. We too often forget that, in reality, being known and understood is a *process* that rightfully can take a lifetime.

Why? Because we're not static creatures. You and your husband each will grow and change throughout your lifetimes—take new jobs, start new friendships, pursue new hobbies, develop opinions on current events, and mature spiritually. You also will make new discoveries about yourselves and understand more about who you are. It's important to share these new discoveries with one another. When one of you begins to feel that the other isn't keeping up, the problems start. He seems to be tuning you out—not wanting to hear about your latest brainstorm, idea, interest, or hobby. You don't want to continue to be treated with indifference, so you have stopped sharing with him. After all, why show an interest in his hobby if he's not going to show interest in yours? Why listen to his opinion if he isn't going to listen to yours? The gulf between you begins to widen, and stress begins to develop. As that gulf continues to widen, communication can be shut down.

Think about your husband for a minute. What do you know about him? Sometimes a woman's knowledge of her husband stops shortly after they get married because she thinks she already knows him. For example, you know your husband's favorite foods, the type of clothing he likes to wear, his favorite cologne, his favorite TV shows. You know a lot about him, but that very knowledge can cause familiarity to set in. You may not feel that you need to learn more—or that there is any more to learn. However, getting to know a person is an ongoing task; you need to keep your "husband database" updated if you want to constantly be sure that you are connecting with him.

So what new information might need to be updated? Has your husband found some new interests? Is he following a new sports team—or does he have information he could share with you about changes on his favorite sports team? What's going on at work? Are there any new employees? Any new exciting projects? Any concerns? What book is he currently reading? What magazines does he like? What does he think about events happening in your town, state, nation, or the world?

Of course, you want your husband to keep his "wife database" updated also. But be willing to make the first move and show your desire to connect with him without asking for anything more in return. You are the one who feels that the current state of your relationship is a problem, so you need to take responsibility for beginning to solve it. And you might be surprised at how quickly he catches on.

UNDERSTANDING
PRODUCES INTIMACY

Showing interest in each other's worlds will create and keep a connection between you and your husband. To have true intimacy, however, sharing more deeply from your hearts is required. Not every husband is skilled at this. Learning to talk about hopes and joys, fears and sadness can take time. Women sometimes equate the effort someone new makes to understand us with being loved. While being understood doesn't always insure intimacy, intimacy is very difficult without it.

That's why there is danger in seeking another person to understand you *in the place of* your husband. *Understanding produces intimacy.* You will begin to feel closer to the person who is listening to and understanding you, and you will feel increasingly distant from your husband. When relational and emotional needs are consistently met by one other person outside of your marriage, the temptation toward a physical relationship is sure to occur.

This helps us see why Susan was at risk for an affair. She was first at risk when Philip, in a very insensitive way, brought a problem to her attention, and *she shut him out rather than talking about it.* Perhaps when they were dating, he had interpreted her willingness to understand football as a willingness to connect with him through sports. Working out together at the gym would have been a way to do that now. Philip's comments about Susan's body were hurtful, but Susan *didn't talk to him about that either.* Instead, she stubbornly avoided both issues.

To Susan, Matt seemed to understand her better than Philip, and that created a sense of intimacy between them. When was Susan first in danger of trying to get her emotional needs met by Matt? When she agreed to go with him to lunch. Matt offered the comfort and reassurance that Susan desperately needed, and Susan willingly accepted it.

RED FLAG: *When you are not with the other man, do you find yourself thinking about him and wondering what he is doing?* ≋

Susan and Philip seem to have some "irreconcilable differences," but that's what drew them together in the first place! Now they both need to give a little and find ways to reconnect *through* those differences and, in the process, get to know each other in deeper and more fulfilling ways.

WHEN CONVERSATION STOPS

Temptation can also be much more subtle. Look at what happened to Lizzie when conversation with her husband stopped.

■ Lizzie and Dan recently celebrated their fourteenth anniversary by going out to a nice restaurant where, as always, they talked about the kids. *It happens every time,* thought Lizzie. *I really don't know what else to talk about. We lead such separate lives.*

Dan has his own home redesign business and spent the last five years building up his customer base. He works out of the house, but he is busy all day and most evenings and weekends. Lizzie respects his desire to make a go of the business, but she often feels that the business is more important to him than his family. And despite how hard he works, Dan makes only about half of Lizzie's salary, and the cash flow is very inconsistent.

Lizzie also works long hours at her job. She works full time in order for the family to have a steady income and health insurance coverage. When she gets home around six, she makes dinner for everyone and then starts on chores. About ten, she drops into bed and falls asleep instantly. She has to get up at five the next morning to be ready to catch the 6:20 train into the city. She can't remember the last time she and Dan were intimate.

Lizzie longs for conversation and understanding. She wants Dan to recognize how hard she works, to thank her for carrying the lion's share of the financial responsibility, to maybe even apologize for not holding up his end. It isn't that she is mad at him or that she begrudges having to work. She likes her job and enjoys having a place to use her skills. It's just that Dan doesn't seem to appreciate what it takes for her to do what she sees as his responsibility. She is out of bed at five; he can sleep till seven. He works from home but never bothers to throw in a load of laundry or start something for supper. And he never asks how he could help her out.

Their boys are six and ten—fun but lots of work. Both are active in sports, and Lizzie sometimes feels that all she does on weekends is drive. Dan sometimes drives the boys to a practice, but it still falls to Lizzie to maintain the schedule and oversee all the details.

A few years ago, the family moved so that Lizzie could be closer to the train. Lizzie discovered that most of the women in her new neighborhood stay home or work only part time. Her next-door neighbor, Debbie, also works—but only three mornings a month doing payroll for a small company. Lizzie envies her greatly. Debbie has time to attend a health club and have a personal trainer (and it shows), as well as time to volunteer at her children's school. Lizzie doesn't have that luxury.

Debbie's husband, Sam, also has his own business, but his is very successful. And somehow, Sam manages to be home quite a lot. Sam has expressed concern for Lizzie on a couple of occasions because she works so hard and such long hours. When their younger kids ended up on the same softball team, Lizzie and Sam started hanging out a bit. Debbie hated softball and skipped the games, and Dan was usually working.

RED FLAG: *Do you feel the need to keep your relationship with the other man a secret?* ≡

As the season progressed, Lizzie began looking forward to the games more and more because she knew she would see Sam. They sat with their lawn chairs next to each other and after a while took turns bringing each other snacks. On the cooler days, Sam showed up with a nice hot cup of Lizzie's favorite Starbucks drink.

"So how did things go at work today?" Sam often asked.

"Well, this project we're working on is facing a tight deadline, but the client just isn't getting back to us with feedback. I'm a bit worried about being late."

"What's the project?" Sam always wanted to know more.

And so it went. Lizzie told him about her clients, her coworkers, her projects, and her concerns. Sam was fascinated with her work and amazed at her talent. It wasn't like she was trying to blow her own horn; Sam just understood the ins and outs of business and recognized Lizzie's professionalism and talent. "I wish Deb would get a job," he said one day. "She spends so much time just hanging out with friends, having lunches, or going shopping."

Not only did Sam appreciate Lizzie's talents, he also understood her time pressures. He often was willing to take her boys to practices along with his own when he knew her time would be tight.

Their conversations ranged from belching boys to quantum physics to welfare reform. One day, when they were discussing local taxes and speculating on the next presidential election, Sam did a perfect impression of one of the candidates, and Lizzie laughed till she cried. Before she could wipe away the tears, Sam had his handkerchief out and started dabbing gently at her cheeks, gazing into her eyes.

Lizzie looked away quickly, but then looked back. She glanced away again. Sitting there in public, she didn't want to betray what she was feeling. Sam was a much better man for her than Dan could ever be.

Lizzie's marriage has been in danger for some time. She has lost respect for her husband because he isn't "holding up his end" of their partnership, and they are no longer communicating because there is no time and, seemingly, little interest. ■

Despite the problems in her marriage, Lizzie wasn't looking for someone else! In fact, if she had been asked about the possibility of infidelity before she met Sam, she would have probably laughed and wondered how she could have time to add one more thing to her life! But even though Lizzie's life is full of activities, it is empty at the same time. Although her life *looks* safe, there is very little real connection with her husband, and with her husband virtually absent, there is no one to encourage her, support her, and affirm her hard work and the contribution she is making to the family.

But Lizzie also isn't taking time to connect with Dan and find out more about his business, his hopes, his dreams. Angry at Dan because of his neglect and the limited income his business produces, Lizzie has chosen a passive response rather than taking steps to try to reconnect with Dan.

RED FLAG: *Do you have sexual fantasies about the other man?*

All these issues together have made Lizzie vulnerable to a friendship that started "innocently" but has the power to damage not only Lizzie's life but also the lives of Dan, Debbie, Sam, and all of their children's lives as well. That anniversary dinner at a nice restaurant could have been the place for Lizzie to gently raise the issue of why there was so little to talk about and what changes could be made to have more overlapping interests. Difficult issues need to be discussed, such as the long-term impact of Dan's business and whether both Lizzie and Dan are carrying equal family responsibilities. Perhaps Lizzie doesn't want to hurt Dan, but he needs to know that his inattentiveness and neglect are jeopardizing their marriage and putting Lizzie at risk for an affair. If Lizzie doesn't feel comfortable raising these issues in conversation alone with Dan, she could look for a safer context in which to do so, with a trusted pastor or Christian counselor to help.

FRIENDSHIPS WITH WOMEN

Until your marriage heals and begins to meet your need for understanding and intimacy, realize above all that you are responsible for finding other God-given ways to have those needs met. Friendships with other women can be one of those ways, but seek to have a variety of friendships, not just one. Take a look at what happened to Donna.

■ Donna and Tom have been married for twenty-five years. Their children, all in their early twenties, have left home for college or to begin a career. Together Donna and Tom raised good kids, worked hard, and put away enough money for a nice retirement. They've survived many difficulties and stuck together, but the spark between them is gone.

Donna had looked forward to the empty nest years, hoping that the newfound time and freedom would allow her to travel, explore the world, and try some new hobbies. But life isn't turning out that way. Donna is bored. Coming home from work every night to a quiet house and no one but Tom...well, it isn't exactly a dream come true. She doesn't see any hope for the future.

Tom wants his routine, his old neighborhood, even the same thing for breakfast every day. He can't understand why Donna wants to try new things. He is happiest when every day is the same as the last. Donna and Tom have been to marriage counseling repeatedly, and it always helps for a while, but Tom loses interest. The bottom line is that Tom doesn't want to have to meet Donna's needs—if he even understands what they are.

A few months ago, in an effort to add some romance to their relationship, Donna asked Tom to take dance lessons with her. He agreed, but almost every week when it came time for the lesson, he found an excuse not to go. Finally, Donna started going without him. The class had more women than men, and some of the women took the men's parts so everyone could dance. That's how Donna met Tracy.

Tracy liked the way Donna danced, so they partnered up. When the first dance session ended, they signed up together for a Latin dance class. Tom didn't care as long as he didn't have to go. Donna loved the class. It was great exercise, and the two hours flew by. She and Tracy chatted in between practice sessions and got to know each other more. They had a lot in common. They both loved learning new things, and Tracy had done a lot of the world traveling Donna hoped to do—Peru, Singapore, Italy, and her next destination was Australia. Tracy encouraged Donna to consider coming with her.

RED FLAG: *Would you feel awkward if your husband were present during your conversations with the other person.* ≋

When the Latin dance class ended, Donna began meeting Tracy for dinner after work once a week. Their relationship grew and deepened. Tracy didn't share Donna's faith, but she had a fascination with spirituality and appreciated it in Donna. The women laughed together about Tom. Donna's stuffy, old-fashioned husband became the topic of many conversations, and Donna realized just how little she had in common with Tom and how much she had in common with Tracy. She began to wonder if she even needed to stay in her marriage. Life could be so much more, so much better, she thought. She felt a deep, affectionate attraction for Tracy. It was as if she was in love. But Tracy was a woman!

Donna tried different ways to deepen the connection in her marriage and increase intimacy, but her attempts were unsuccessful. Tom sabotaged her efforts. Donna was discouraged and vulnerable when Tom stopped going to the dance lessons that Donna hoped would produce intimacy. Donna's choice was difficult—to continue with an activity that brought her pleasure or to stop and confront Tom with his lack of involvement with her.

Perhaps continuing an activity with another woman felt safer to Donna than confronting Tom. Maybe it never crossed her mind that her need for intimacy was being met by another woman. But because understanding produces intimacy, a relationship with another woman also can be seductive and can threaten your marriage. That's why it's important to have several female friends you connect with, not just one, and why it's never a good idea to allow a relationship with a best friend to take precedence over your relationship with your husband.

THE TRUTH

Finding Solutions

Susan, Lizzie, and Donna all had problems in their marriages that created vulnerabilities for them. However, they each chose to get their needs met through someone other than their husbands. *Actively seeking intimacy with your spouse is God's desire for you.* You and he are to be "one flesh" (Genesis 2:24). Fighting for your marriage includes fighting for a deeper relationship. Passively staying in a marriage and resigning yourself to the way things are is *not* a healthy plan.

Start your search for solutions by being realistic—no other person will ever *completely* understand you. It takes a lifetime to know someone intimately, and it takes willingness on your own part to be vulnerable and honest in every area of your life. When someone new enters your life, who seems to be "better," who seems to understand you—this person cannot really know the depths of who you are in such a short amount of time, and you do not know this person completely either. To think that ultimate knowing and understanding is actually happening with this new person is foolish. Don't fall for it.

So how do you handle the deep need (and sometimes even the wound) inside you that your husband's lack of understanding creates? Our culture labels this "incompatibility" and encourages you to get a divorce. How many divorce decrees have the tag line "irreconcilable differences," yet even the best marriages are *filled* with irreconcilable differences! Part of a successful marriage is finding out what makes each other tick and then, because of your love, making those irreconcilable differences work *for* you!

Connect with God

As adults we are responsible for getting our needs met. God wants you to let *Him* meet your needs first of all. The more you get your deepest needs met by God, the freer you are to love and connect with your husband without demanding that *he* meet all your needs.

And because God is the only one who can truly know you and understand you completely, to ask your husband to do that is unfair. Perhaps he could do better than he is doing now, but stop and ask yourself this: *Am I expecting my husband to be God?* Only God can be God. Scripture says,

> O LORD, you have searched me
> and you know me.
> You know when I sit and when I rise;
> you perceive my thoughts from afar.
> You discern my going out and my lying down;
> you are familiar with all my ways.
> Before a word is on my tongue
> you know it completely, O LORD.
> You hem me in—behind and before;
> you have laid your hand upon me.
> Such knowledge is too wonderful for me,
> too lofty for me to attain.
> Where can I go from your Spirit?
> Where can I flee from your presence?
> If I go up to the heavens, you are there;
> if I make my bed in the depths, you are there.
> If I rise on the wings of the dawn,
> if I settle on the far side of the sea,
> even there your hand will guide me,
> your right hand will hold me fast.
>
> —PSALM 139:1–10

God also says that He knew you before you were born, and He calls you by name. He already knows everything about you, and He loves you anyway. He wants you to get to know Him better so that you can fully experience His love. You can trust Him completely. If you're having difficulty in your marriage because your husband doesn't understand you, let your husband off the hook for a while and deepen your relationship with God.

Connect with Others

One of the marvelous aspects of an ongoing relationship with God is that He provides healing for you as you connect with Him *and* with other people. God created us to live in relationship with Him and with others. We need safe relationships with other people in our lives.

The important distinction here is that you need *people*—not just one person. As we've already seen, looking to one other person to fill the needs that your marriage is not meeting is not safe. But connecting with a group of healthy, mature friends will go a long way toward meeting your needs for understanding and intimacy. You'll become a more complete person and be better able to connect with your husband unselfishly even when the situation is difficult.

Here are a few ways you can begin to connect with others:

Don't keep your struggle and pain to yourself. Share what's going on with a trusted friend or counselor.

Join a group. It might be a Bible study, MOPS, or a growth group of some kind.

Reach out and serve others. Volunteer in your community.

God's wonderful promise to us in James 4:8 is that if we draw near to Him, He will draw near to us! The only one who can ever completely know and understand you is God. Don't expect your husband to be God. Let him just be your husband and let God be God. Then ask God to renew your love for your husband, and work hard at getting to know your husband better. You may be surprised what you learn!

take action

First of all, if any of the red flags throughout this chapter exist, it is time to take action—immediately! Even if the attraction to the other person is mainly in your mind and the other person is unaware of your feelings, the red flag is still flying and calling you to action. For our own well being and the well being of those we love, the Bible encourages us look for the way out of temptation that God promises to provide (1 Corinthians 10:13). Here are some concrete steps to take:

✓ Immediately put some distance in your relationship with the other person. Adjust your schedule to find ways to avoid this person—in other words, do the opposite of what you've been doing. If the other person wonders why, explain that you're a married woman committed to working on your marriage, and let the conversation end there.

✓ If you cannot avoid the person completely, you can "cool" any unhealthy emotional connections by including your husband in some of the interactions. (For example, Lizzie could make sure that Dan comes to some of the softball games so that she is no longer alone there with Sam.) Recognize that even if your behavior has not yet "crossed the line," you are in danger and need to change the relationship.

✓ If the relationship has already crossed the line to emotional or physical intimacy, it's time to get help and not try to manage the situation by yourself. One of the best ways to do this is to find another woman you can trust, perhaps a mature Bible study leader or a godly counselor, and tell her about your temptations and concerns.

✓ If your marriage is not meeting your needs and you are tempted to get your needs met in another relationship, it's time to actively seek God in stronger and deeper ways. Again, if you are unsure about how to do this, find a spiritual mentor to help you.

✓ Some first steps you might take are joining a women's Bible study, setting aside time for reading God's Word and for prayer, and writing Bible verses on note cards to carry with you and read over when you are tempted to think of the other person.

Lie #5

He's just my friend;
there's nothing wrong with that.

Joan always had lots of male friends. She grew up with four brothers—two older and two younger—and she has always felt comfortable around guys. Feminine, but strong and athletic, Joan was willing to try just about anything, and she could usually do whatever she tried. Whether it was rock climbing, waterskiing, or hiking, Joan could keep up with the guys.

She also could hold her own as an armchair quarterback. Her brothers played most sports, so she knew the terminology and the rules, and she could spot a bad call as quickly as anyone.

RED FLAG: *Do you lack female friends?* ≋

As a result, Joan usually found herself hanging out with guy friends. She had a few girlfriends, but she usually ended up annoyed with their incessant talk about clothing, hairstyles, and makeup. She was always much more interested in who would be going to the Super Bowl and which players would be starting.

Don found Joan fascinating. He'd never met another woman who was so much fun! In the spring of their sophomore year at college, in the middle of the baseball stadium, right on the pitcher's mound, Don got down on one knee and proposed.

They were married that summer and moved into a small apartment near campus. Their apartment became the place where the guys came over to watch the big game. It didn't hurt any that they used their wedding money to buy a big screen TV just for that purpose!

Don's pre-med major began keeping him busier and busier. His tough classes and lab projects often meant he got home late at night. Joan had more free time, and she continued to host game-night gatherings at their apartment. Twice Don came home late to find several guys lounging around their apartment or the mess the guys had left behind.

RED FLAG: *Do you have male friends you spend time with apart from your husband?* ≋

Crawling into bed beside Joan after the second party, Don asked, "So you had a party, huh?"

"Of course, it was Packers and the Bears tonight! Everyone wanted to see the game. Don, you should have seen it! The refs were terrible! I couldn't believe this one call in the third quarter..." But Don wasn't listening. He'd assumed that Joan wouldn't host gatherings without him. He fell into a fitful sleep.

Don decided not to mention his feelings, but the next week when he saw that Joan was preparing for another Monday-night-football gathering, he spoke up. "Joan, I won't be able to be here tonight. You know I have to make a presentation tomorrow, and my lab partner and I need to prepare."

"That's all right. I wish you could be here to enjoy the game, though. We'll miss you. Hey, I need to get to class and then do some shopping. I'll catch you later. Good luck on your prepping." With a peck on his cheek, she was gone.

The following week, it was the same, except this time Don vowed to get home earlier. He walked in the door to find four guys he'd never met sitting on his couch watching the game.

"Hey, babe!" Joan yelled from the kitchen. "Patriots are ahead!"

Don contained himself until he got to the kitchen; then he spoke in a low whisper. "Joan, who are these guys? I've never even seen them before."

"Oh, just some New England fans feeling lonely for home. I know one of them from sociology class; the rest are his buddies. I invited them."

"We need to talk," Don said as he walked out of the room and into the bedroom.

RED FLAG: *Are there areas in your marriage where you resist compromise or change? If yes, are you defending deeply held values or are you resisting some of the "becoming a couple" that happens in a marriage?* ≣

After all the guys left, Joan closed the door behind them and then found Don. "What was that all about? You sulked in here the entire evening and missed a great game!"

"Joan, I'm just not comfortable with you having a bunch of guys over to hang out when I'm not here."

"You've got to be kidding! That's what you're upset about? Come on, Don. We've always had people over. They're just guys. They're my friends from class. Good grief. Don't you trust me?"

"It's not that I don't trust you, Joanie. I don't trust them. I just don't think you should have parties with guys, especially guys I don't know, when I'm not here."

RED FLAG: *Are male friendships meeting needs for you that your marriage should be meeting?* ≋

But Joan wasn't convinced. In fact, she was angry. How dare he put a crimp in her social life just because he was busy with school! It was just a bunch of friends watching football. Besides, these were the guys who asked her for advice about their girlfriends. They saw her as their buddy.

As time passed, Don and Joan became angrier with each other. Joan refused to stop having parties; Don became more and more distant because Joan wouldn't do as he requested.

One evening only one guy showed up for the party—a diehard Seahawks fan had come to see the game. Joan found herself enjoying his company immensely. They had a lot in common, including growing up with lots of brothers. At halftime, Joan found herself confiding in Randy about her marriage, the growing lack of intimacy, the anger she felt toward Don.

Randy continued to come to the game nights, but he and Joan usually weren't alone. Joan really wanted to continue to build this friendship, so she and Randy began to plan lunches away from campus where they could talk. Randy took her anger seriously and—more important—sided with her about the house-party issue. If he were in Don's shoes, he said, he'd be more understanding.

Joan continued to have sports parties. Don refused to attend even if he was free, so Randy played host along with Joan.

It wasn't long before their friendship became an affair. They were able to keep it a secret until one evening when Don came home late and found the two of them cuddling in the kitchen after cleaning up. Later that night, Joan admitted to the affair, hoping to hurt Don.

Joan and Don started counseling together in hopes of saving their marriage. But Joan saw her only fault as letting her friendship with Randy get out of hand. She didn't understand why she couldn't continue to keep her male friends. Otherwise, she feared, she would have no friends at all. ■

BONDS OF FRIENDSHIP

One of the wonderful gifts of friendship is not facing life alone; we have company on the journey and, although we don't know what might happen on that journey, we know we have friends to share it with.

From an early age, friendships help us learn how to treat someone else respectfully, how to share burdens, how to receive help as well as how to give it, and how to stay connected in community. When we are isolated, it is easy to begin to believe that something is wrong with *us* and that our situation is worse than it really is.

We share ourselves in friendships. In healthy same-sex friendships, we open up and share our lives with other women we trust and value. In other words, we become vulnerable as we reveal who we are. Our friends "return the favor," and our lives are richer as we get to know another person. We can't predict if a family member will become ill, if we will lose our job, or if we will experience physical or emotional problems, but when problems occur and we share them with a friend who is there for us, the intimacy increases. And when we take time to be available for friends, those friendships also deepen.

Friends naturally take our side. You are fortunate if, when you confide in a friend about a difficulty in your marriage, your friend encourages you to hang in there and also to get help. And you can offer the same support when the roles are reversed.

When you are single, it is very appropriate to have both male and female friends. Male friends help us understand and appreciate life from a man's perspective and bring a dimension of balance to our lives. Having a variety of male friends and dating for friendship rather than for romance is a good way to learn about the character qualities that you want in a husband. After you are married, however, good boundaries in opposite-sex friendships are essential.

The love and care you have for your friends naturally is expressed through hugs, visits, calls, deep sharing, and help. Emotional intimacy develops. However, when your friend is someone of the opposite sex, you risk having an intimate connection that will threaten your marriage, whether that intimacy is expressed physically or not.

A safe boundary when you are married is to not spend leisure time alone with another man. Instead, work at developing friendships with other couples and groups of couples. If your husband has single female friends or if you have single male friends, both of you should be present when they are around.

LIFESTYLE CHANGES

Ideally, marriage involves being concerned about each other's thoughts and feelings and together building a lifestyle that accommodates each person's needs and desires. Sometimes, though, we resist this process, choosing instead to retain our freedom to do whatever we want, despite our husband's unhappiness. The result is that our marriage never becomes all it should be. Instead of a married couple, we are two "married singles."

When Joan met and married Don, she didn't see a need to change any of her habits or activities; she continued to act as she had when she was single. She chose to ignore and then dismiss her husband's feelings of discomfort and, later, jealousy. Don also had concerns for Joan's safety and told her clearly he worried about her being alone with guys he didn't know. But Joan disregarded his feelings and asserted her independence.

Marriage, however, needs our commitment to serve our spouses even when to do so goes against our own desires. The apostle Paul wrote to the Christians in Galatia, "You have been called to live in freedom... But don't use your freedom to satisfy your sinful nature. Instead, use your freedom to serve one another in love" (Galatians 5:13, NLT). About marriage specifically he wrote, "A married man is concerned about the affairs of this world—how he can please his wife.... A married woman is concerned about... how she can please her husband" (1 Corinthians 7:33–34). The best marriages enjoy mutual submission: "Now as the church submits to Christ, so also wives should submit to their husbands in everything. Husbands, love your wives, just as Christ loved the church and gave himself up for her to make her holy, cleansing her by the washing with water through the word" (Ephesians 5:24–26).

One way to test the impact of your behavior is to ask yourself how you would feel if your husband behaved in a similar fashion. How do you think Joan would have felt if Don were hosting all-girl parties when she wasn't home?

Another good question for Joan to consider is why she didn't seek out other women who enjoy watching and participating in sports, since many do. Perhaps, growing up, Joan enjoyed the status of being the only girl able to hang out with the guys and speak their language. Maybe having other girls present who also enjoyed sports and understood the games represented competition for her and undermined her self-image as a female "cool enough" to hang out with the guys. Now, as an adult, Joan could learn about herself and grow as a person by exploring these questions.

Spending time with men as friends felt familiar to Joan, but once she was married, she should have made a point of finding women friends who shared her interests. There was no good reason for her to restrict the sports nights to men only.

FRIENDLY CONFIDANTS

When Joan and Don began to have problems, Joan had a set of ready-made friendships with guys in whom to confide. One man in particular was receptive and provided reassurance and understanding that Joan felt she was no longer getting in her marriage. Beginning with verbal expressions of understanding and reassurance, the friendship slid into physical expression and became an affair. This is not an uncommon occurrence.

Confiding in friends of the opposite sex about problems in your marriage is a recipe for trouble. Again, Joan needed female friends to talk over her problems with her. And it's always important to examine your motives when you share problems in your marriage with outsiders. Are you looking for sympathy, vindication, or attention? Or are you seeking godly wisdom from mature women whom you trust? Talking about problems is the right thing to do, but talk with the right people and with the right motives. Paul wrote, "We are each responsible for our own conduct" (Galatians 6:5, NLT).

MODELING LESSONS

A friendship with a man other than your husband can be a way you choose to mask your insecurities rather than deal with them directly. And the results, as Maddie found out, can be disastrous.

■ People are rarely surprised to find out that Maddie is a model. She is statuesque, toned, and striking. Her straight white teeth, clear skin, and long dark hair make her look more like she's twenty-two than the mid-thirties wife and mom she is.

Maddie got into modeling as a child. She never became famous, but her modeling gigs helped put her through college. While many of her friends were taking out loans and working hard during the school year, with just a few photo shoots Maddie had enough money to pay her bills and then some.

Oddly, Maddie's good looks didn't make her popular in college. She actually was fairly shy, except in front of a camera. And she was so good looking that most of the guys she met at school either thought she was unavailable or were just too intimidated to ask her out. Finally Maddie met Bruce, a quiet guy—some might call him a nerd—who studied computer technology and worked nights as a paramedic. Bruce thought Maddie was clearly out of his league, so he never tried to impress her; he just was himself, and Maddie liked that. Eventually they began to date, and they got married soon after graduation.

Within five years, Maddie and Bruce had three children. Maddie loved her kids, but she was frustrated by the effect on her body of three pregnancies close together. Her modeling days were over. To boost her self-esteem, Maddie worked whenever she got a chance, but otherwise she devoted herself to establishing her home and raising her children, getting involved in their school activities too.

Bruce was a great dad and a good provider. His expertise in computers landed him a high-paying job, and he still enjoyed working as a paramedic on a very part-time basis. But he was a quiet guy. He loved Maddie but didn't always know how to express it. To him, she was absolutely perfect; he didn't sense that Maddie struggled with self-esteem issues or worried about losing her looks. He always told her she looked great, but somehow Maddie didn't believe him. Looking in the mirror at her less-than-perfect abs, she only remembered how great she used to look in a bikini.

RED FLAG: *Do you and your husband have little time alone together?*

About five years ago, the children's school was putting on a spring fair as a fund-raiser, and Maddie found herself on the committee. The idea was to offer games and activities with prizes in various rooms throughout the school. One room would have a professional photographer. Maddie was asked to contact one of the dads who worked as a photographer.

The first time she called Stan, they clicked. They spoke the same language—she knew all about camera angles and lighting. Together they talked about some great ideas to draw the kids in—costumes and settings for some fun pictures. In the course of the conversation, Maddie told Stan about her background as a fashion model. They shared a few "war stories" about bad photographers and arrogant models. Maddie realized how much she missed being in front of the camera. "But I've had three kids and am way past all that now," she joked.

When Stan and Maddie met on the day of the fair, Stan was stunned at her beauty and told her so. Maddie was flattered. Somehow it meant more to her to have Stan say it than Bruce—after all, her husband was supposed to say it; Stan was an outsider and a professional photographer who was supposed to see flaws and problems.

At the end of the day, Stan casually mentioned that he would like to photograph Maddie, and Maddie couldn't resist. They set up a time, and Maddie wondered if, with a new portfolio, she might be able to get back into modeling part-time.

And that's just what happened. The pictures opened up doors with several agencies who worked with older models. Maddie felt like a new woman.

At first Bruce reveled in her success and at being married to the beauty who began popping up in various print advertisements, but slowly he became annoyed at the amount of time Maddie was away from home. Maddie assured him that the extra money was worth the short-term sacrifices and that her modeling was going to put the kids through college, just as it had done for her.

RED FLAG: *Do you keep your professional life entirely separate from your family?* ≡

On one weeklong shoot, Stan turned out to be the photographer. Maddie loved posing for him, and it brought out a side of her she had forgotten—the sensual, exciting side. It wasn't long before Stan's constant proximity, attentiveness, and affirmation of her beauty weakened Maddie's resolve to keep their relationship completely professional. They became close friends. That lasted for a time until their "harmless friendship" became an affair that lasted for four years.

Bruce remained unaware of the affair the whole time. Maddie always defended her "friendship" with Stan based on how important his connections were to her career.

But when Stan accepted a transfer and moved away with his family, Maddie became seriously depressed. Bruce discovered the affair and left her. Maddie was devastated by the reality of the damage she had done. She has spent the past two years recovering from depression and the guilt that resulted as a consequence of her "harmless friendship." ■

Our culture associates many characteristics with physical beauty. What attributes do you associate with an attractive man or woman? Self confidence? Assertiveness? High self-esteem? Maddie possessed none of those characteristics; in fact, her beauty hid her insecurity. Her modeling actually gave her a persona to hide behind rather than providing her with ways to develop the immature parts of herself.

Maddie and Bruce were both shy people; although their outer appearances didn't match, they matched beneath the surface. After they were married, each of them continued to keep their insecurities to themselves. Neither was able to develop enough trust and safety with the other to share what was really going on inside, and so their marriage suffered. Maddie became quietly depressed; Bruce remained unaware and unbelieving that someone who looked as wonderful as Maddie could be suffering with depression and issues of low self-esteem.

The busyness of a young family can cause both husband and wife to slip into parenting roles and neglect spending time together nurturing their relationship. Becoming a child-centered couple is also a way to avoid the problems that exist in yourselves and in your relationship. With three children in five years, Maddie struggled with a complete lifestyle change. She didn't take much time for herself or for her relationship with her husband.

When Maddie resumed her professional life, she kept it very separate from her family. She was able to compartmentalize her work life so completely that she wasn't able to see how her relationship with Stan was hurting her marriage. Unfortunately for this couple, when the deception that accompanies an affair came to an end, Bruce was not willing to continue with the marriage, and so it ended. Maddie was clearly unaware that she had been putting so much at risk by pursuing a friendship with Stan.

Maddie initially went to counseling about ongoing depression and anxiety. At first, she referred to the tension within her marriage but did not mention her sexual relationship with Stan. Later, when she did disclose the affair, she was amazed to discover that there was a link between her emotional issues, her marital tension, and her infidelity.

STRUGGLING FOR SURVIVAL

Sometimes when a couple experiences problems, one of the spouses adamantly refuses to seek help. That puts the burden of getting help on the other spouse, and not just for the marriage, but for herself. As Leticia learned, however, the company of a male friend is the wrong place to look for help.

■ Leticia and Will have been struggling for some time. They've been married just a few years, but it seems to both of them they've been unhappy the whole time. Yet they didn't start out that way.

When they met in college, they seemed like a match made in heaven. They enjoyed working on projects as a team. Leticia was enthusiastic, and Will was good at follow through. They laughed easily and enjoyed each other's sense of humor. They had the same political bent, the same ideas about religion, and even the same taste in movies. They liked to go to the local library to check out old movies or foreign films with subtitles. They once organized a marathon Sunday at the movies where everyone watched all six Star Wars movies in order; it was a huge success.

RED FLAG: *Are you and your husband loners, without some good couple friends that you both enjoy?*

When they got married, Will's job moved them to a new part of the country, and their social life became each other and their old movies. That was great for a while. They liked just being together, making some popcorn, and settling in on a Friday night to watch *The Philadelphia Story* or *Breakfast at Tiffany's*.

Leticia got a job working as a receptionist. Things seemed to coast along fine until, two years into his new job, Will discovered that he was being laid off. The combination of the layoff, the fact that they had not yet developed any close friendships in their new location, and the uncertainty of the future spun Will into a depression. As the darkness deepened, Will withdrew, becoming less communicative. When his job ended, he simply sat all day in front of his computer.

RED FLAG: *Have you neglected to become part of a supportive church?*

Leticia tried to help. She suggested that Will go for counseling, and that medication might help. She pleaded with him to start attending church. She thought about hosting a movie party as they had in college and inviting some neighbors. But the depression had taken such a hold on Will that he couldn't summon the energy to think about it, and Leticia let the idea go.

Through coworkers, Leticia discovered an artsy movie theater in a nearby city that ran all kinds of offbeat movies—art films and foreign films with subtitles. Thinking a simple night out would help, she planned a date with Will and did get him out to see a movie. The next morning, however, Will was back under the dark cloud again. Leticia didn't know what to do. She was becoming angry because Will wouldn't take control of his life, and she felt completely alone.

RED FLAG: *Are either you or your husband depressed? Is this affecting your marriage?* ≡

At work one day, Leticia made plans to go to the artsy theater again, this time with the coworkers who had told her about it, Megan and Roger. Soon the three of them were often going out after work for a movie and then dinner at a nearby diner, where lively discussion always followed. Then Megan began dating someone and wasn't free after work, but Roger and Leticia continued their movie dates. Will rarely questioned Leticia when she got home late. He hardly seemed to notice that she'd been gone.

Eventually, Leticia realized she was spending more time with Roger than with Will. But what difference did it make? Will was uncommunicative, depressed, and never interested in sex. He slept a lot.

Leticia worked as much overtime as she could. She handled the bills, the shopping, the cleaning, the laundry—all the little details of life. Will did virtually nothing. She hadn't signed on for this—Will was the detail guy; Will had always taken care of these things. She hated doing it and wasn't very good at it. But she gritted her teeth. If she didn't do it, it wouldn't get done.

The nights out at the movies were her reward to herself for the load she was carrying. Roger was a caring friend and a good listener. He even helped her do her taxes—something Will had always handled before.

One night, Roger and Leticia attended one art film that was especially erotic—and it had an effect on the single man and the sex-starved lonely wife. After the movie, instead of going to dinner, they went back to Roger's apartment. Leticia felt guilty, but she justified her behavior with the rationale that her husband wasn't satisfying her. If Will gets his act together, she reasoned, I'll give up the relationship with Roger. For now, Roger is just taking the pressure off Will.

Will hated not being in control of his situation. He always had a plan and was happy when the plan came together. Being laid off was not part of his plan. Not knowing what the future held, he was overwhelmed by his fear and he felt immobilized, unable to function. ■

Depression is an illness, not just feelings of sadness or "being down." Listlessness, inability to concentrate, feelings of low self-worth, and changes in sleeping and eating habits are all signs of depression. While Will's depression seems to have been triggered by his life circumstances, he needs professional help to begin functioning again. The good news is that depression is treatable and responds well to a combination of therapy and medication. Although the changes in Leticia's husband were drastic, they will be reversible once he begins getting help.

Leticia's situation would have been very different if Will's sudden change in functioning had been caused by a head injury or by a disease process more difficult to treat. But Will's refusal to get help for his depression put the marriage at risk. The less he did (under functioning), the more Leticia did (over functioning), until she was carrying all the responsibility and Will was sinking deeper into depression.

Their situation was even more strained because they did not have any good friends in their current location to turn to for help. Leticia could have enlisted the support of old friends or family members to encourage Will to get help, but she did not, and she was left carrying the burden alone.

Unfortunately, the member of a couple who needs help often refuses to find or accept it. When one spouse has an obvious problem, the "healthy" spouse often focuses his or her energy on getting the "unhealthy" spouse into treatment. But like Will, many spouses resist, which fuels the tug-of-war. Leticia did encourage Will to get help, but she did not try to find help for herself. She needed some ongoing counseling for dealing with a depressed spouse and processing what changes to make for herself. Just as the spouses of those with addictions need help, often the spouses whose mates are refusing to get help for a mental illness need support as well.

Eventually Leticia gave up and found other relationships to meet her needs. By taking energy out of the marriage and focusing it on a friendship with Roger, she *felt* better. But her connection with Will continued to weaken as she was handed all the responsibilities at home, and it weakened even more when the friendship with Roger became an affair.

All affairs (whether with people, with your career, or with a consuming activity) are essentially triangles. The tension between two people becomes too great, and often one brings in a third party to "stabilize" the situation. Think back to junior high when you had a falling out with a close friend. One of the first things you probably did was call *another* friend and enlist her sympathetic ear.

While this strategy may have relieved the tension for you then, it did little to solve the issues between you and your close friend. An affair functions much the same way. While it may make you *feel* better, it further damages the marriage and guarantees that the original issues creating distance between you and your husband will remain unresolved. To put it another way, Leticia's affair with Roger took some of the pressure off her marriage *and* allowed Will to remain depressed.

THE TRUTH

"He's just my friend; there's nothing wrong with that" is a lie. When you become engaged and marry, individual friendships with men other than your husband should change dramatically. Those friendships should no longer be exclusive and should not be your primary sources of emotional intimacy. They should never be substitutes for emotional intimacy between you and your husband.

Clearly, God values friendship. Scripture speaks to the importance of friendship with verses like these:

A friend loves at all times, and a brother is born for adversity (Proverbs 17:17).

He who loves a pure heart and whose speech is gracious will have the king for his friend (Proverbs 22:11).

The heartfelt counsel of a friend is as sweet as perfume and incense (Proverbs 27:9, NLT).

As iron sharpens iron, so a friend sharpens a friend (Proverbs 27:17, NLT).

If one falls down, his friend can help him up. But pity the man who falls and has no one to help him up! (Ecclesiastes 4:10).

The LORD would speak to Moses face to face, as a man speaks with his friend (Exodus 33:11).

Jesus chose twelve men to live closely connected with Him during His ministry. On the night before His death, Jesus told them, "I have called you friends, for everything that I learned from my Father I have made known to you" (John 15:15). Among the twelve, Peter, James, and John were Jesus' best friends; they were the three He asked to keep watch while He prayed in the garden before He was betrayed (Matthew 26:37–38). And Jesus had both male and female friends. In the account of the death and raising of Lazarus (John 11:1–44) is tucked this little verse: "Jesus loved Martha and her sister and Lazarus" (v. 5).

Because human beings—man and woman—reflect the image of God, we are intended to live in relationship with one another. "In the Lord,...woman is not independent of man, nor is man independent of woman. For as woman came from man, so also man is born of woman. But everything comes from God" (1 Corinthians 11:11–12). We need each other. That's one reason why, for example, men and women who are single enjoy being included in gatherings and events with their married friends and family. Yet Scripture is clear about how we are to treat and to regard members of the opposite sex other than our spouses. Paul wrote to Timothy, a young minister, "Treat...older women as mothers, and younger women as sisters, with absolute purity" (1 Timothy 5:1–2).

When two people marry, one does not *complete* the other. Marriage involves two whole people coming together to create an entirely new entity, their marriage. Although in your marriage you become one, you do not cease to exist as yourselves. Friendships with others outside your marriage should continue to be important to each of you but within the boundaries that Scripture has made clear.

Friendships that would come between you and your husband are out of place after you are married. Becoming a couple means making adjustments and sacrifices for the sake of the new "one"—your marriage—and for the sake of your spouse. Paul wrote in his letter to the Christians at Ephesus:

> Wives, submit to your husbands as to the Lord. For the husband is the head of the wife as Christ is the head of the church, his body, of which he is the Savior. Now as the church submits to Christ, so also wives should submit to their husbands in everything.
>
> Husbands, love your wives, just as Christ loved the church and gave himself up for her to make her holy, cleansing her by the washing with water through the word, and to present her to himself as a radiant church, without stain or wrinkle or any other blemish, but holy and blameless. In this same way, husbands ought to love their wives as their own bodies. He who loves his wife loves himself. After all, no one ever hated his own body, but he feeds and cares for it, just as Christ does the church—for we are members of his body. "For this reason a man will leave his father and mother and be united to his wife, and the two will become one flesh." This is a profound mystery—but I am talking about Christ and the church. However, each one of you also must love his wife as he loves himself, and the wife must respect her husband. (Ephesians 5:22–33)

take action

✓ In your marriage, do you feel like a couple? Are you happy to have your husband by your side? If not, why not? What thinking needs to change on your part? What might you need to discuss with your husband?

✓ Assess your friendship support network. Do you need to spend more intentional time cultivating and encouraging friendships with other women?

✓ Do you and your husband need to develop friendships as a couple with other couples? Discuss this with your husband and make a list of a few couples to invite over or to double date with.

✓ Are you a supportive friend? Do you have a supportive female friend?

✓ If there is a man other than your husband whose company you enjoy, limit your interactions to group activities. If this feels restrictive to you, ask yourself what needs you are seeking to meet through this relationship.

✓ Assess your work friendships. How much does your husband know about the people (especially the men) with whom you work? How can you begin an open dialogue about that so he is included in and not separated from your work life?

✓ Do you have female friends who share your faith? If you were in trouble of any kind, would you feel comfortable calling them and talking about what is happening? Could you ask them to pray for you? If not, what can you do to develop this kind of friendship?

Lie #6

The man at work is more exciting than my husband. I'd be better off with this other man.

Marjorie is a highly trained, well-respected professional in a very demanding, male-dominated industry. Her husband, Mike, is also successful in his field and a solid employee for his company. Mike is one of those guys that everyone likes. He's friendly, outgoing, easy to talk to, always helpful. By contrast, Marjorie likes to challenge the status quo, and as a result she finds herself in conflict much of the time. The men in her office, while appreciative of her abilities, describe her as "tough as nails" or with other less-flattering terms.

Mike and Marjorie met and fell in love in college, and even though both of them had been raised in nominally Christian homes, they began having sex not long after starting to date. After graduation, motivated partly by love and partly by guilt, they got married and settled into a fairly typical two-career marriage. Fifteen years later, they both still work hard and are climbing the corporate ladder; Marjorie, driven as she is, has climbed a little higher than Mike.

RED FLAG: *Is there unresolved guilt over your sexual involvement with your husband before you were married? Did you get married "to make it right"?*

Romance, however, is just a distant memory. Marjorie and Mike have settled into a polite, socially respectable but loveless marriage. Mike says—half in jest, but with more than a trace of bitterness—that their three kids must be the products of immaculate conception. When asked in a counseling setting how often they are intimate, Mike says, "We have three kids, so...." Sex is not really an issue or an argument; it's just nonexistent. The passion they had felt before marriage is gone.

Mike cares very much about Marjorie and would like to save their marriage. "Let's move to the country," he has suggested numerous times. He'd like to find a place where life is less frantic, where their stress level can come down a few notches, and where they can focus more on family and on each other. But Marjorie won't even listen. "Are you out of your mind?" she asks every time he brings it up. "I'm finally getting to the top level at the company. It hasn't been an easy climb, Mike. You know that. I'm not going to walk away now!" She thinks about how the men at her office would smirk while she cleaned out her spacious office in order to follow her husband to the middle of nowhere.

The last time they had this conversation, Mike shrugged his shoulders and smiled. "I'm proud of you, Marj, I really am. I just think our marriage could use some work." When he reached over to give her a peck on the cheek, she turned away. *Follow this guy to the boonies? No way,* she thought bitterly. *That's not where my life is headed.*

RED FLAG: *Do you and your husband have common goals and dreams?*

A few weeks later, Marjorie sat in on an executive meeting as the CEO droned on with his weekly report. Suddenly an item on the agenda made her sit up and take notice—the name of the new hire coming in as a vice president. He had been Marjorie's boss at another company, her first job. She remembered with a slight blush how much she had fantasized about him then, even though she was engaged to Mike. Steve was brilliant, savvy. He was going places. Now he would be here! Marjorie was excited to see him. They had made a good team at the time, and she looked forward to working with him again.

His first day on the job, Marjorie was overjoyed. Steve seemed genuinely pleased to see her. As the other men in the office groveled for position with "the new guy," Marjorie already had an in.

Things couldn't have been better. Because Steve and Marjorie had worked together before, they knew each other's styles. They worked in tandem on several projects; they each seemed to know what the other was thinking. They were equally driven to perform top-quality work and to do whatever was necessary to make that happen. Late nights at the office became the norm.

"So Steve, did you ever get married?" Marjorie asked over a slice of pizza one night as they waded through proposals and estimates.

"I did, but it didn't work out," he said with a bit of sadness.

"I'm sorry..."

"That's okay. She and I were just too different. I really needed to focus on my career to get to the position I wanted. She never understood the long hours or the constant calls. One day I received divorce papers at the office. When I got home, she was packed and gone.... What about you? Tell me about your family."

"I have three great kids—two teenagers and a preteen and all pretty busy. One plays basketball, one's on the speech team, and one has a telephone permanently attached to her ear."

"And your husband?"

RED FLAG: *Do you confide in coworkers of the opposite sex that you are having marriage problems?* ≋

"Well, Mike's a great guy. Everyone likes him because he's so easy going. But that's just the problem. He's so easy going he's driving me crazy. No drive, no laser-beam focus. His latest kick is to try to talk me into moving to some hick town, 'far away from all the busyness,' he says. You might as well kill me as take me away from civilization. To tell you the truth, I'm sort of thinking of a separation."

She stopped. She pretended to stay focused on looking through files on her laptop, but she was assessing the impact of her words. She wondered what Steve would do with the information that she was thinking of leaving her marriage. He did not seem to react to the news, and Marjorie continued to look at her computer screen. Her stomach was churning—either from the excitement or maybe the late-night pizza, she wasn't sure which...

"I need both of you on this trip," the CEO requested the next day. "This client trusts you both but wants to see you face to face before he signs on the dotted line. I need you both there tomorrow."

Marjorie dashed home, threw together her suitcase, and left a note about the kids' schedules for Mike along with a promise to call after her meeting the next day.

In the hotel lobby in the morning, Steve and Marjorie had coffee and then headed off to the meeting. Confident but a little worried at the same time, they discussed how to make the deal happen.

Their meeting with the client was like a finely tuned tennis game— lob the conversation back and forth, fill in for the other at the right times, decide with a glance who would answer each question, show that they were a team to be counted on. The client was so impressed that he signed the contract and then began discussing future projects.

At the end of the day, Steve and Marjorie decided to celebrate over dinner. Walking into the restaurant beside Steve, Marjorie was reminded of all her old fantasies. She never even thought to call Mike as she had promised—in fact, she never thought about Mike at all. After dinner, in the elevator at the hotel, Marjorie took Steve's hand, and in her take-charge manner pushed the button for her floor, making it clear that she wanted him to stay with her, to make physical the emotional connection that they had experienced all day.

The excitement of sex with this man she so admired, so connected with, was beyond anything she had ever experienced with Mike. ■

Working outside the home is a necessity for many women, and many other women choose to work as a stewardship of their gifts and talents for God's glory. But it can be challenging to keep work relationships—especially those with male coworkers—healthy and God honoring. In order to protect her marriage, a woman who works must be able to realistically assess her priorities, her motives, and her relationship with her husband. She also needs her eyes wide open about the special challenges to marriage that workplace relationships can create.

THE ENERGY EQUATION

There is an emotional energy created by doing a job well, meeting a deadline, or reaching a goal. Experiencing this energy can spill over to your marriage in a positive way. When you feel good about yourself and what you are doing, you have more energy for interacting with your husband and children during the hours you spend with them.

But doing a good job at work can demand and drain energy

too. We all have only twenty-four-hour days. Whether the energy equation of your job works *for* or *against* you and your marriage is an important consideration. Whether you are working to help support your young family, to save for your children's college bills, or simply to use your skills and be salt and light in your community, it's important to take a good look at the energy you are investing at work in relationship to the energy you are investing in your marriage and family.

Job-related stresses can challenge any marriage. While we are called to be accountable to the Lord for how we use our gifts and talents, our work is never meant to replace our relationship with the Lord or our relationship with our families. Treating our co-workers with respect and caring is a time-honored way to advance in our careers. An important "gut check" is to ask ourselves if we are treating our family members in the same way. Do you listen at home with as much care as you listen at work? Do you show respect for the opinions and needs of your husband and family members? It is too easy to give so much of our time and energy to a work setting that we have very little to give at home.

MOTIVES MATTER

Your career may provide financial benefits or insurance coverage your family needs. It may well be the best way for you to use and develop the skills, talents, and abilities that God has given you. But take a good look at *all* the reasons you are working—they may not all be positive.

Regardless of why you went to work in the first place, you may have different reasons now. Even the most engrossing and challenging profession is still what we *do*, not the definition of who we *are*. Our identity remains in Christ, and we are His. But sometimes women find that they are not clear about who they are. Do you see yourself as "only" a mom? Are you shaky in the self-esteem and confidence department? If so, the success and positive reinforcement you experience at work can bolster your insecure identity. Before long you find yourself working primarily for the sense of self-worth that a career provides you. Your identity becomes bound up in your job.

But God says that our self-worth comes from Him. He tells us, "I have loved you with an everlasting love; I have drawn you with loving-kindness" (Jeremiah 31:3). He clearly showed that love when He bought us back for himself at an incredible price, the life of His Son (1 Corinthians 6:20). If there's a problem with how we view ourselves, we need to ask God for His help and direction rather than turning to our career to fill the void.

A woman also may invest in a career as an escape, a way of avoiding difficulty and pain in her marriage. Certainly it is easier to turn our attention to what we are good at, to what is going well, to what makes us feel comfortable, and to turn *away* from what is difficult and *un*comfortable. But in the long run, the losses caused by this approach will be much larger than the gains.

A question to ask yourself is: "Am I focusing on my career because God is leading me to do so or to avoid spending time on my relationship with my husband?" To answer this truthfully requires that you honestly assess your marriage on a regular basis.

THE STATE OF YOUR UNION

Intimacy in a marriage is a result of many factors, including shared experiences and time spent together as well as shared goals, dreams, and values. Physical intimacy can suffer when you have little emotional or spiritual intimacy with your husband. If your marriage lacks intimacy in any area, acknowledge this and seek help. Intimacy deficits in your marriage make you prey for the lie that a more exciting man at work is the answer to your situation.

Unresolved guilt over premarital sexual activity can interfere with your desire to be sexually intimate with your husband or with your ability to enjoy that relationship. Don't be afraid to admit to your past; instead, bring it before the Lord for His forgiveness and healing so that you can enjoy a satisfying sexual relationship with your husband now. Taking this step for yourself and for your marriage is an important safeguard for women in the workplace.

THE ALLURE OF THE WORKPLACE

A work environment can provide a place for two people to get to know each other, develop a friendship, and start to move toward more emotional intimacy. Coworkers often spend more time with one another than with their own spouses in conversation and sharing details of everyday work life. Shared problems, jokes, and stories can create a feeling of warmth and closeness, and this becomes especially dangerous if these feelings are absent in a woman's marriage. One definite sign that a work relationship is becoming too intimate is confiding in someone of the opposite sex about the problems in your marriage.

In addition, the workplace makes it easy for a false perception to flourish: the perception that two coworkers truly know each other well. It's easy to think that you know someone well when you are involved with him on a project, spending a lot of time together, combining your talents and ideas. Together you experience the shared excitement of working hard toward a common goal and the exhilaration of success. Even a shared failure bonds you together when you console each other.

But each of you really only knows who the other person is *at work*. You see each other as well dressed and confident and able to handle any problems that arise. You don't lack for anything to talk about because you have so much work-related information in common. Your connection is very one-dimensional. It leaves out the other important areas of life—family and connection with God.

You probably guessed the ending to Marjorie's story. Misplaced priorities, mixed-up motives, and a marriage without intimacy all help us see why Marjorie began an affair with Steve that ended up destroying her marriage.

Early into her marriage, Marjorie began to focus most of her energy on her career; her marriage received only whatever energy was left over. Her relationship to her husband wasn't a priority. She did not give her marriage the attention it needed to be maintained, let alone to grow. Have you ever asked your husband to tell you what *he* thinks about the impact of your career on your relationship with him? How would Mike have answered that question if Marjorie had asked?

Another issue for Marjorie and Mike was that their sexual relationship in marriage was burdened with their guilt over their sexual activity while they were dating. Their "solution" to having not honored sexual boundaries while dating was to get married; they never dealt with the underlying problems. They needed to find a way to seek God's forgiveness and to forgive each other for their premarital sexual relationship so that it didn't continue to be a source of hidden pain in their marriage.

Marjorie's relationship with Steve was so exciting because, as with most affairs, Marjorie had the ability to edit her relationship with him. In other words, this was a relationship built around the false perception of knowing someone well. One-dimensional relationships can seem exciting for a while but ultimately cannot satisfy.

How different this story might have been if Marjorie and her husband had taken time for their marriage, taken responsibility for healing past hurts, and established some jointly shared goals and dreams to work on as a couple.

POSITIVE AND NEGATIVE

Sometimes we need to come to terms with the "negative" counterparts of the positive traits that drew us to our husband initially. Otherwise we can be deceived by relationships in the workplace that look like what we really want instead of what we think we've got. Here's what happened to Ann.

■ At thirty-five, Ann married Harold, fifteen years older and a widower who had lost his wife many years before. Harold is old-fashioned and very much the gentleman. He has worked hard to get to his position in life and now is settled, dependable, predictable. And Ann fell in love with him. When they began to socialize (Ann would have just said "dating"), she often teased him about his old-fashioned ways and tried to shake him up a bit. Ann saw it as a personal challenge to bring the sun back into his dreary life.

Harold fell for Ann too. She indeed made his life brighter. Every time he saw her, his heart swelled with feelings he hadn't experienced for a long time. He couldn't believe that Ann wanted to be with him. He felt the years fall away whenever she walked beside him and took his arm. Her laughter and charm delighted him.

Ann had waited a long time to get married because she'd seen too many of her friends stumble—or leap—into unwise or disastrous marriages, some that had not survived. So when she met dependable, stable Harold, when she saw that she could light up his dreary life, she decided to propose to him. Of course, being the old-fashioned guy he was, he made her wait until he could do the proper proposal his way.

They seemed like perfect counterparts. His stability and dependability complimented her vivacious passion. The home they built was fully paid for (his stability) and decorated with beauty and vibrant colors (her passion). They worked together on church committees—she brought new and exciting ideas, while he brought fiscal responsibility and the take-charge mentality that could bring those ideas to fruition.

But just a few years into the marriage, despite what looked perfect from the outside, Ann and Harold could see what was beginning to crumble from within. Their problems first surfaced in the bedroom. Her passion drove her ideas about lovemaking—ideas that were very different than his. She desired spontaneity, creativity, and (of course) plenty of passion; he wanted familiarity, even predictability. The frequency of their lovemaking suffered, as did their level of satisfaction. He was irritated by her seemingly constant need for sex and her desire to be spontaneous at a time when he hadn't "planned" on having sex. Ann tried to back off a bit; Harold tried to be more spontaneous. But somehow, in the end, the passion was lacking.

So Ann began to pour her passion into her work. A creative

consultant for an advertising firm, she threw herself into her creative tasks, putting her natural drive and energies to good use. Her job became her fulfillment.

One day Ann literally ran into Jerry coming around the corner from the copy machine. Jerry was a natural flirt, and Ann had been at the receiving end of his compliments many times. She had laughed him off—he was just this side of sexual harassment, but he never crossed the line. He was younger than most of the women in the office, who all considered him harmless. Intensely creative, he dressed with flair and could always be counted on to say clever things. Passion sort of oozed out of him—passion for his projects, his job, his life.

"Hey, great job on that piece for the O'Brien account!" he said after they apologized for practically bowling each other over.

"Thanks," Ann responded. "I felt great about that one."

"If you have a few minutes today, I'd like your input on a project I'm stuck on. Maybe if I talk it through with someone, it will get some creative juices flowing."

Ann looked quickly at her watch. "Sure, I'll come by in ten minutes. I have a lunch meeting, but that gives us about half an hour."

RED FLAG: *Is your career a threat to your marriage? (If you are not sure about this, ask your husband!)* ≋

"Great," Jerry said with his winning smile and headed back to his office.

As they talked, Ann found that Jerry really appreciated her input— and not only appreciated it but also used it in the final form of his project. When he was lauded by the company for his results, he pulled her in beside him to give her credit for her part.

Ann began to find excuses to go to Jerry's office—inventing questions, having a story to tell, making up something she needed to find out. And it seemed that he was just as eager to talk with her as she was to talk with him. He often spontaneously stopped into her office and invited her to the cafeteria for a cup of coffee. She never hesitated to join him for a quick break.

RED FLAG: *Do you have business meetings alone with a male coworker because it is necessary or are you using work as an excuse to spend time alone together?* ≋

Ann began to think about running away with Jerry. She daydreamed of the exciting life they could have, traveling the world, opening their own business, making love behind a closed door at the office...then she'd shake herself. C'mon, stop it, Ann. You're a married woman. He's a boy. But try as she might, she couldn't help what she was feeling inside. He was so interesting, so spontaneous, so creative, so much fun to be with. And late one afternoon, when they were alone in his office laughing about the latest office gossip, they happened to lean close to each other and in a flash, Jerry kissed her. Even though she wanted to continue, she pulled away, but she knew he could see how much she wanted him.

The next morning, lying in bed beside Harold, Ann was overwhelmed with conflicting feelings. Kissing Jerry had been spontaneous and passionate—everything she thought she wanted. She felt like a door had been opened, and she desperately wanted to walk through it. She knew she wasn't ready to deal with the crushing load of guilt she would face if she did. But she knew she couldn't continue on the way she was going much longer.

The traits that attracted Ann to Harold before they married became problems for her after they were married. But Harold hadn't changed after the marriage; he was the same person he had been always been. What changed was Ann's perception of Harold's dependable nature and lack of spontaneity. ■

In her book *After the Affair*, Janis Abrahms Spring calls this the "flip-flop factor." We all have traits that serve us well in one situation and not in another. For example, the person who is independent, confident, and self-reliant may also be perceived as cold, distant, and unloving. Or the person who is thoughtful, accommodating, and caring may also be seen as unassertive, ineffectual, and weak.

Valuing the positive traits in our husbands is easier when we are dating; after marriage, in order for us to continue to value those positive traits, we may be required to come to terms with their negative counterparts. We will have a more difficult time doing this if we struggle with those same negative traits in ourselves. Ann had a cautious side, demonstrated by her reluctance for many years to get married. When she was single, perhaps she had trouble being as spontaneous as she was free to be after she married Harold. Perhaps it was Harold's dependability that gave Ann the anchor she needed to be even more creative.

Part of Ann's motivation for marrying Harold was the influence on him she thought she could have. Wanting to change Harold and brighten up his life may have set her up for failure. We can't change another person, much as we would like to; we can only change ourselves. We can certainly request different behaviors from our husbands, but true change is up to them. Ann will continue to feel that her marriage is a failure if she measures her success by the changes her love produces in her husband! Her challenge is to love and accept Harold as he is, rather than how she hopes he will become.

Finally, Ann will need to stop demanding spontaneity from Harold. Making demands, rather than requesting what we would like, can often bring out negative traits in our husbands. Requiring spontaneity from Harold in their sexual relationship is not getting Ann the results she desires. She needs to focus on the aspects of the relationship that are working well and encourage and compliment Harold for those. That will empower him to be more creative *when he chooses to be.*

Somehow Ann has not learned how to enjoy the differences between Harold's personality traits and her own. She has unknowingly set up what could remain a no-win situation by being attracted to Harold's steadiness and dependability and then asking him to change those very traits after marriage. Rather than address this issue head on, she has chosen to "settle" and turned to the workplace to look for the satisfaction in life that she longs for.

YOU AND ME AGAINST THE WORLD

Marriage difficulties can bring a couple closer or they can drive the couple apart, depending on the choices the two people make as they deal with the difficulties. Take a look at what happened to Ellie.

■ Ellie and Jake have been married just over six years. They've known each other for as long as they can remember, attending the same schools in their small town. After graduation, Ellie went to a community college in a nearby city for a degree in interior design; Jake attended a technical school for auto mechanics across the state. After two years, they were both back in their hometown. Ellie could not find a position in interior design, so she began working at the local Wal-Mart and in a downtown diner, while Jake signed on at the auto repair shop up on the main highway.

Ellie wanted to get married and start a family. When Jake sat down at her counter for lunch one summer day, he and Ellie rekindled their high school friendship. Jake, too, was ready for the next stage of life. They dated for about five months. Everyone in town knew about their budding relationship, and the pressure to go ahead and "get hitched" was more than a little intense. Jake and Ellie obliged with a lovely Christmas wedding.

Their first few years of marriage were volatile. Making ends meet sometimes was a struggle. Still young, Ellie and Jake needed to figure out the process of paying bills, handling work and marriage responsibilities, and accepting each other's differences. But though they sometimes argued, they also had fun making up!

For a couple years, they rekindled some of their old high school friendships, inviting people over to their apartment to watch the game or the latest video. But they became increasingly concerned about those friends—irritated by their "small town gossip mentality" and concerned about their views of right and wrong. Ellie and Jake wanted to find Christian friends they both could enjoy, but their little church was filled with mostly older people. Finding a new church in a neighboring town would be difficult for Jake, especially, because he was essentially an introvert. The people at their church would be upset also—and Ellie and Jake didn't want to cause trouble. So they just stayed, week after week, feeling more and more isolated. Instead of drawing them together, the isolation became a wedge between them. They blamed each other for the aloneness—Jake blamed Ellie for being too picky about their friendships; Ellie blamed Jake for being afraid to look for a new church.

They began going different directions. Jake joined a bowling league with his buddies to give him "something to look forward to every week." Then he added a poker night and the Jaycees to his schedule, and suddenly he was busy several nights a week. Determined not to stay home alone, Ellie began hanging out with some of her old girlfriends—doing whatever they were doing just to get out of the house. She enrolled in an exercise class at the local Y—and she began working the night shift at Wal-Mart.

Working at the store late at night was a very different experience. A few customers still roamed the aisles, but the employees could kick back a bit and enjoy themselves, while still getting their job done. But a few funny comments over the intercom, a pizza party served in the eating area, and lots of light banter were the norm. Ellie loved it!

Then she began noticing Paul—or rather, she began noticing how much he was noticing her. They made small talk, teased back and forth, and often found ways to work in the same aisle in order to continue their chatter. He was so much fun to be around, and Ellie couldn't wait to get to work at night. She'd leave before Jake was back from his evening activity and get home after he left for work in the morning. She was having the time of her life!

Because she and Jake so rarely crossed paths, Ellie felt increasingly disconnected from him. If she arrived home a couple hours later in the morning, he'd never know. So Paul and Ellie started planning breakfasts out. It was innocent at first. They were just great friends. Even so, half the fun was trying to keep the friendship a secret—it was like they were Bonnie and Clyde planning their getaway after they both punched out in the morning. They'd find a way to meet up in a town several miles away where they hoped they wouldn't be recognized. The more they talked and laughed, the more intimacy they felt, and the less careful they were. But Ellie didn't care—or at least she didn't think she cared. Although she wasn't ready to admit it, she was starting to have feelings for a man who was so much more fun and interesting than Jake! And the secrecy only made it that much more exciting! ■

RED FLAG: *Are you consistently experiencing the emotional energy that comes from working together with just one person rather than with a team?* ≋

Work relationships can have the advantage of seeming legitimate. Who's to say whether your interactions with a coworker are work related or not? At first, only the two individuals involved know when a relationship has emotionally crossed the line. Unfortunately, even the excitement produced by having a relationship that looks safe but isn't adds to your feelings of connection.

Ellie definitely crossed the line when she and Paul began to plan their breakfast getaways without including other coworkers. Sharing meals often generates feelings of closeness and connection. In addition, the playfulness with which Ellie and Paul approached their breakfasts added to their growing feelings for each other.

Ellie and Jake understood the importance of good friendships to a healthy marriage, but they didn't know how to find them. Instead, they each went looking for fun and friendship apart from each other.

THE TRUTH

We've examined the lie that "the man at work is more exciting than my husband. I'd be better off with this other man" and have seen that the work environment provides specific challenges to maintaining a healthy marriage.

Work provides a way for us to use our gifts and talents; it meets our needs for achievement and satisfaction and allows us to bring in needed income for our families. But work also can be an energy drain and an escape. Our desire to do a good job or to be seen as competent and responsible can cause us to spend more time at work than necessary or wise.

It's easy to fall into finding our identity in work rather than in what God says about us, and work relationships can create an appealing sense of intimacy and connection that can seem very real. In addition, how someone appears in the work setting may not be an accurate picture of what that person is really like. At work, we present our "best selves" more consistently than in the relaxed privacy of our homes.

One truth that combats the lie that we would be better off married to the person at work is that we don't really know what it would be like to be married to the person at work! If Marjorie marries Steve, then *she* will be the spouse outside the work setting waiting for Steve to get home from a business trip! She only knows Steve in one context—work—and not what it would be like to be married to him. If Ann marries Jerry, she no longer will have the strength and security that she receives from Harold. She doesn't really know what Jerry would be like as a husband, only as a coworker! Jerry, with his flighty spontaneity, may be completely inept at running a home, paying the bills, and planning for the future. All that Ellie really knows about Paul is that he is "fun." She doesn't really know what daily life with him would be like at all.

At its core, the lie that someone else is more exciting and therefore better completely ignores any sense of God's plan for us. God knows our wounds and our weaknesses and every detail of our situation, and He knows when temptations will enter our lives. He willingly gives us grace, strength, and resources to deal with all of these when we ask and are ready to follow His paths for our lives. He says:

> "I know the plans I have for you," declares the LORD, "plans to prosper you and not to harm you, plans to give you hope and a future." (Jeremiah 29:11)

God promises to give you the desires of your heart when you commit yourself to Him. Psalm 37:4 says:

> Delight yourself in the LORD, and he will give you the desires of your heart.

We need a strong connection with Him so that His relationship of love with us shapes the desires of our hearts, rather than those desires being shaped by other influences. Understanding how much God loves you and being committed to living life His way are truths that will steer you away from the deceptions of the workplace that can destroy your marriage.

take action

✓ Take some time alone in prayer with a journal and ask God to show you His plans for using your talents and gifts. The Latin word *vocare* means "calling," and while we usually use "calling" to indicate God's leading into full-time Christian service or ministry, in fact all work can be done for His glory! "Whatever you do, work at it with all your heart, as working for the Lord, not for men" (Colossians 3:23).

✓ Review your work-related goals with your husband and invite him to do the same with you. Be each other's encourager, supporting the ways that God is guiding each of you to use your talents and gifts in the workplace.

✓ Be intentional about having conversations with your husband concerning each other's work environments. Learn each other's challenges, fears, and successes.

✓ Pray for your husband based on what you know about the challenges he is facing at work, and ask him to pray for you in a similar way. Pray together about these things.

✓ If you are aware of an attraction to someone at work, be sure you limit—or better yet, eliminate—time alone with him. If the attraction continues to be a problem, it might be necessary to find another place to work!

✓ Be sure you are seeing your work as a way of serving your marriage and your family, rather than the reverse. If we put our work before our marriages, we are in danger of losing both.

✓ If you sense that a coworker or boss has an interest in a more personal relationship with you, intentionally bring your husband and your connection with him into your conversations with this person. Also be sure to remain professional and appropriate in all your words and actions throughout every workday.

✓ Attend all of your husband's work-related social events and ask him to go with you to all of yours. Others' seeing your husband as a "real person" can be a protection for you in the work environment.

✓ In the book *The Seven Principles for Making Marriage Work*, author John M. Gottman encourages spouses to use "poor baby" conversation as a way to connect with each other after work. In this conversation, spouses always take their partner's side when their partner talks about the workplace. Sometimes the reality of not being a part of your husband's work setting frees you to be wholeheartedly supportive of him!

✓ Remind yourself that you are "working for the Lord, not for men." Choose a small object that symbolizes your commitment and place it in your office where you will see it every day.

Lie #7

No one will ever know.
I can end this anytime.

Sue and Will seemed a bit like an odd couple, but the pastor was completely unprepared for what Will was about to say.

Will was one of those solid, stable church members—always there on Sunday morning, Sunday evening, and Wednesday night; always could be counted on to help with a building project or Vacation Bible School; always there to set up chairs in the fellowship hall and put them back after an event. Will's wife, Sue, was usually around on Sunday mornings only—and then only if she wasn't working. She seemed to have a busy schedule, and Will usually made excuses for her absences. But Sue was friendly enough and seemed very engaging when she was around. People liked her.

The pastor sat down in his armchair and motioned for Will to sit on the couch. "Will, tell me. What's wrong?" he began.

"Sue is having an affair."

"What? Are you sure?"

"I've seen her! I had been having some suspicions—like why she always seemed to have to go out of town so often. She used to go to some daylong training meetings once in a while, but recently it's been almost every week. Then I got this phone call from a woman who said she was leaving her husband because he was having an affair with my wife! I thought it was a crank call and tried to dismiss it, but things just weren't adding up.

"I had yesterday off, so I borrowed a friend's car, and I followed her. I actually went to her parking lot at work and parked way off to the side. I saw her leave work about ten in the morning and I followed her car. Gee, I felt like some detective on TV. It was awful. After about a twenty-minute drive, she pulled into the parking lot of a seedy-looking motel. I drove by and then came back and parked in a parking lot nearby. I saw her come out of the motel office and unlock one of the doors to a room. I sat in the car with my heart in my throat. It was all I could do to sit still. About five minutes later, this guy pulled in and parked beside her car. At that point, I didn't recognize him. She opened the door and let him in. He went inside for forty minutes, and then he left. She came out twenty minutes later and drove away. I was so crushed and hurt and mortified that I couldn't move. I couldn't believe this was happening! Instead, I just sat with my hands gripping the wheel and tears running down my face."

"Will, I'm so sorry. You said you didn't recognize him at first. Do you know who he is now?"

"Yeah. The guy works with my wife—actually works for her, I think. Pastor, how could I have been so blind? And now what do I do?"

"Sometimes we get so wrapped up in the busyness of life that we fail or neglect to observe what is happening around us. Does Sue know that you know?"

"Yeah, I confronted her last night."

"And?"

"At first she denied it. Then I told her that I had followed her. She broke down and told me she never intended for me to find out and that she was going to break it off. Pastor, we need help. Will you see us?"

They set up an appointment for the next day. The pastor told Will that he would need to hear Sue's account of events, and Will agreed. When Sue and Will arrived, the pastor met briefly with them together and then asked Will to step outside the office while he talked with Sue.

"Sue, I want to hear your side—"

The words were barely out of his mouth when Sue began to talk. "Pastor, Will is a wonderful man. I never intended to hurt him. He is kind and stable, a hard worker and a good provider. This whole thing started with just a little harmless flirting. I always thought I could control it.

RED FLAG: *Are you bored with your life? With your relationship with your husband?* ≋

"Then Shawn became kind of exciting. The continual flirting began to break me down, and things just happened. I never thought I'd get caught. I thought I could break it off anytime and everything would go back to normal. Will is just so stable and predictable. I needed more excitement in my life.

"I did try to break it off about three months ago, but Shawn threatened to tell Will and file a sexual harassment suit against me—I'm his boss. I felt trapped into continuing the relationship. I won't call it an affair; that's too degrading. It was just supposed to be fun between two friends. I never thought I'd get caught. I never have before. I figured we'd slowly get tired of it, he'd move on, I'd be free of him, and no one would ever know."

"What do you mean, you never have been caught before? Have there been other affairs?"

"No, just some little things I've kept from Will. I have a couple of credit cards he doesn't know about."

"How could he not know?"

RED FLAG: *Is there no one who holds you accountable for your actions?*

"I handle all of the finances, and the bills for the credit cards are sent to me at work. Will doesn't know about them. I've been using the money from our son's college fund to make the payments, and I'll just repay that when the cards are paid off."

"How much do you owe?"

"About thirty thousand dollars."

"What?"

"It was up to thirty-five thousand, but I've paid some of it off."

"How did you get that far in debt?"

She sighed, as if for the first time actually seeing the numbers for what they were. "Well, I made a couple of loans to Shawn. I paid all the motel bills. But I also bought my kids a lot of clothes and Will a few nice things. He just figured I paid for them. Plus I need new clothes all of the time for work."

RED FLAG: *Do you keep financial secrets, or other secrets, from your spouse?*

"Is there anything else I should be aware of? You realize that in order for this marriage to be saved, you and Will are going to need to come clean and be completely honest with each other."

"Yes, I realize that."

The pastor called Will back in. Sue came clean about the financial issues. Will was devastated, but Sue insisted that it was no big deal; she would pay off the credit card bills. She also insisted that the affair was no big deal; she expressed regret only that Will had found out. She couldn't understand why they just couldn't pick up where they were and continue on. She claimed that her indiscretions were sins against "God and God only." She doesn't think she needs Will's forgiveness, so she refuses to ask. "It's over," she says. "What more does he want?" ■

WHO, ME?

Sometimes women who are having affairs behave exactly like people who are caught in an addiction—they look to their affair partners to provide a "high" to help them feel better about themselves and their lives. Addicts fear reality. There may be hurtful wounds in an addict's life or background, but rather than facing those honestly, the addict chooses to deal with life in dishonest, unhealthy ways—pushing her realities underground, covering them up, medicating, compensating. The drug might be overwork, ministry, perfectionism, alcohol, prescriptions—or an affair.

Like an addict, a woman caught in an affair practices deception and lives in denial. She believes her own distorted view of reality and resists anyone who tries to tell her the truth. Common distortions that women having affairs persist in believing are: "I can end this whenever I want," "No one will ever know," or, as Sue maintained, "This is not really a big deal. It doesn't mean anything."

When a woman is in denial, she refuses to look at the consequences of her actions. Like an alcoholic who says she can stop drinking anytime, a woman having an affair may insist that she can end the affair and move on whenever she chooses. When she is caught, she resists examining her actions and instead downplays the affair. She blames her spouse, pushing her problem back on him. Like Sue, she claims that she needed more excitement in her life; she refuses to look at her own part in the affair.

Denial also shows up when the affair ends and a woman wants to pick up with her husband right where she left off. Why her spouse is upset and wants a more serious response from her seems beyond her understanding. She feels entitled to her choices and resents her husband, or anyone else, for suggesting otherwise.

HONESTY, THE BEST POLICY

The issues in our lives that cause us to make bad choices in one area also frequently result in problems in other areas as well. Sue's comfort with deception and her assumption that she could live as she wished apart from her marriage created a climate that allowed her to secretly overspend.

For a marriage to be healthy, the two people involved must be honest with each other. Honesty doesn't mean outspoken unkindness, but it does mean revealing to your spouse the truth about you, about your feelings, fears, desires, and actions. "Do not lie to each other, since you have taken off your old self with its practices" (Colossians 3:9). Refusing to be truthful about our thoughts and feelings, or keeping quiet about them, is a type of lying. "A truthful witness gives honest testimony, but a false witness tells lies" (Proverbs 12:17).

Being honest with others requires you to first be honest with yourself. It means facing what you fear; facing your pain, failures, and losses; facing your shortcomings and sins and saying, "Yes, this is reality."

HONEY, I SHRUNK OUR MARRIAGE

If a woman is inclined to live in escape and denial, she likely will find herself denying the problems caused by her affair, just as she tried to deny the problems that led her into the affair in the first place.

Will faces a tough dilemma. His desire to remain committed to his marriage will make it difficult to resist Sue's plan to simply pick up where they were and continue on. But without repentance on Sue's part and a willingness to be honest about what happened, "continuing on" will not provide the stability needed to build a stronger marriage.

Ending an affair, like recovering from an addiction, is a process. First the affair has to end, with no further contact with the affair partner. Then grief must be experienced, as both the lost affair and the damaged marriage are mourned and recovery begins. Finally, the marriage needs to be assessed and rebuilt. This process is not quick and can be quite painful for both partners.

Because the process of ending an affair and rebuilding your marriage can be so painful, the temptation exists to try to quickly put the affair in the past. It seems so much easier to say "I'm sorry" and simply move on with life, rather than going through the painful work of ending the affair, asking a partner's forgiveness, and then together trying to rebuild a stronger marriage. But such a quick escape from the problems created by an affair—and the problems that led to it—doesn't work. Unless you are willing to face your life honestly and address your unhealthy patterns and ways of coping, the problems that led to the affair will lead to additional trouble and destruction in your life.

LOST IN CYBERSPACE

Characteristics of affairs include secrecy, deception, and getting emotional and sexual needs met outside our marriages. An online fantasy life meets those criteria, as Miranda found out.

■ Miranda dearly loves her husband, Alan, and their three-year-old twin daughters, but being a stay-at-home mom is wearing her down. She spends her days chasing the girls, cleaning up after them, potty training, reading the same books over and over again, and talking in simple sentences. She has been starting to feel that her intelligence has been reduced to a level just above that of a cucumber. A former sales director, her sales abilities seem to be quickly disappearing now that the only selling she does is to convince her daughters to eat and take naps.

Miranda has talked with Alan about going back to work, but sales jobs usually require travel, and she doesn't want to be away on long trips. Even if she could find something that didn't require travel, the costs of childcare, commuting, and upgrading her wardrobe would be high. Perhaps when the girls are in first grade, they decided, the time will be right for Miranda to go back to work. But that is at least three long years away.

It might have been okay if Miranda felt that she and Alan were doing well in their marriage, but instead she feels that he is slipping away from her. As she sloshes around in juice and peanut butter and jelly, he is out having interesting lunches with clients. She fears that she is becoming less interesting. After all, what does she have to talk about except what the twins do each day?

Miranda's fears became even more intense after Alan's negative reaction to her idea that they try some of the suggestions she found in a magazine article titled "Put Some Zing Back in Your Marriage." Alan just laughed and rolled over to go to sleep. That night, Miranda barely slept at all.

One day, while waiting in line at the grocery store, she overheard two women describing the personalities they had created for each online dating service they were using. "Why, even married people are doing it," one of them said, adding that it had done wonders for her cousin's marriage. "It's just harmless fun," the other replied. "It's not like having an affair, after all."

RED FLAG: *Are you involved in online activity that you cannot stop?*

The idea rolled around in Miranda's mind. A few days later, while the twins were napping, she was on the Internet when a pop-up ad for an online dating service appeared. "Thirty-day free trial!" it announced. "Click here!" So she did.

One click led to another, and soon Miranda had created her cyber self: Angela, age twenty-four, single, personal trainer. "Angela" enjoyed walks on the beach, country music, and NASCAR racing. Miranda lowered her weight, increased her breast size ("I always wanted to be a D cup!"), and made herself a blonde, blue-eyed bombshell. She couldn't help but laugh as she looked down at her flabby thighs in sweatpants and ran her fingers through her nondescript hair. She could be anyone she wanted! This was amazing. She created a brand-new, sexy persona.

She dropped "Angela" into the dating site's database and waited to see what would happen.

RED FLAG: *Are you allowing online relationships to take the place of connection with your husband?* ≋

Within two days, Angela received messages from several men, and Miranda had lots of laughs. She wrote back to each one. She talked about trips she'd never taken and sports she'd never played. She feigned interest in every man who wrote her. Some wanted pictures, but she ignored those.

More e-mails arrived in her private box on the Web site every day. She couldn't believe there were that many lonely hearts out there. Of course, maybe they also were not who they claimed to be! But then who were these men? Maybe they were happily married too, just looking for a little fun, a little outlet. Maybe they were nuts. Oh, well. It didn't seem to matter. She'd never meet them.

Miranda loved being complimented for her breast size, loved having men fawning over her and sending suggestive messages. In fact, many of the e-mails were quite explicit. She at first deleted those, thinking that was going a bit too far. But the more suggestive e-mails she read, the more she felt that flush of excitement. She began to respond to some of the more explicit e-mails with sexual innuendo. "I'll just be mysterious," she laughed. But it wasn't long before innuendo gave way to outright sexual fantasy discussions with these cyber men. She looked forward to logging on every day and letting her imagination take off.

As the free trial period was coming to a close, Alan and the girls came down with the flu. Miranda was so busy taking care of her family she did not go online for several days. When she finally signed on to her e-mail again, she saw the "thanks for renewing" message from the dating service. She'd forgotten that the trial program had required her to give a credit card number. Her credit card had been charged. *Whew! It's a good thing I gave them my personal credit card number,* she thought, with a laugh. *Wouldn't want Alan to see this!*

"Angela" had a bunch of messages. Michael's was the most intriguing and suggestive. She and Michael exchanged e-mails over the next few days. Then he suggested instant messaging at a specific time. Miranda laughed as she suggested an evening when she knew Alan would be working late.

She logged on that night and began the back and forth with Michael. He got right to the point. His IMs quickly turned from mischievous to explicit, and it was clear that Michael was not merely typing. She decided to try it too, and soon they were having cyber sex, the Web equivalent of phone sex.

Miranda was hooked. She told herself that this was really going to help her marriage because she would be so much more sexy with Alan. And besides, where was the harm? "Angela" wasn't a married woman and she wasn't actually having sex; therefore, she wasn't having an affair. And no one would ever know. ■

Online activity provides an environment that fosters secrecy and maximum deception! When you are dating, you usually work very hard to present yourself in as positive a way as possible. But "dating" online, without any face-to-face interaction, provides even greater ways to distort the truth.

Miranda's online life, like any affair, created a split between her life with her family and her secret life with her online affair partner. Eventually, she may be found out—risk always exists that the boundary between the secret life and the real life will be crossed. Perhaps her husband will walk in unexpectedly and see her e-mail, or perhaps an online affair partner will try to contact her in person. But even if her cyber affairs remain secret, they will still impact her in other areas of her life. She has created more distance and deception in her marriage. She already is depending on the time online to meet her need for excitement and connection, and soon her online activity will seem normal—more normal, in fact, than the other relationships in her life.

Eventually the energy it takes to maintain such a fantasy life will take a toll. Miranda is investing precious energy that she could be using to strengthen relationships with her husband, children, and friends instead of building a clandestine life online.

Miranda did try to address her problems in her marriage with her husband, and he refused to take her seriously. Rather than giving up after just one try, however, Miranda needs to "push back" against his minimizing tactics and let him know how unhappy she really is. Even her first try at communication was less than honest. "Let's put some zing back into our marriage" is a very different message than "I am lonely and unhappy, and I feel like our marriage is in trouble." Remember the Scriptures about honest speech that we listed earlier?

Miranda rationalized what she was doing by inventing another person who "really isn't me." But "Angela" is a disguise, like a costume, to conceal the woman beneath, and that woman is still Miranda. What Angela does certainly impacts Miranda, no matter how much she tries to deny it. We are influenced by what worlds we enter through books, movies, or the Internet. Remember the last time you cried during a sad movie or were inspired by watching a heroine persevere against difficult odds? How long did you carry that experience with you? Was the influence positive or negative in your life? Miranda's secret activity online has had a big negative effect on her thought life.

Even though our thoughts don't "show" the way our actions do, we are responsible for guarding our thoughts, because, as we've discussed throughout this book, how we think determines who we become. "For as he thinks within himself, so he is" (Proverbs 23:7, NASB). We are encouraged by Scripture to "take captive every thought to make it obedient to Christ" (2 Corinthians 10:5). The spiritual battle that we fight against temptation begins in our minds. By conceding that battle and telling herself that her mental unfaithfulness was harmless, Miranda opened herself up to greater temptation, and then she fell for that as well.

JUST PRAY ABOUT IT?

While praying is always the right first thing to do when we encounter difficulties in our marriages, it is not the only thing God expects us to do. When we refuse to be honest about our struggles and refuse to seek help, the results are never good, as Audrey sadly discovered.

■ Audrey is the wife of a prominent community leader. Her husband, John, is the president of a powerful organization with ties to many of the churches in their community, including their own. John has devoted his life to his career and vocation. He truly sees it as a ministry. Unfortunately, John has been so preoccupied with his ministry that he has neglected his wife and children. Audrey says, "John has sacrificed his wife and children on the altar of his ministry." She puts on a good face, however, playing hostess at parties and fund-raisers, shaking hands, smiling, standing behind her man. But she is bitter and resentful, seething and hurting behind her smile. It has been this way for a long time.

RED FLAG: *Is there a large gap between how people see you and how you really are?* ≷

Audrey often cries herself to sleep, sobs muffled in her pillow, not wanting to wake her husband. She loves him; at least she had at one time. But the hurt is intense. She feels so neglected, so alone. He is a giant of a man to everyone else, but he is shrinking in her eyes. She hates that. She wants to feel important to him. She longs for those early days of their marriage when he continued to court her with flowers and the touch of his strong hand.

Audrey prayed earnestly for her husband. She prayed that he would be successful, but also that he would somehow sense that his family needed more of him. He is seen by everyone in the community as the mentor, the go-to guy, the super-Christian. But who is mentoring him? Who is holding him accountable? No one. She begs God to bring someone into his life who can help him see that blind spot.

But the years went by and the heavens were silent. It became more and more difficult to keep praying. Audrey saw her children go from elementary school to junior high to high school with no more input from dad than they'd ever received. She wondered if God had heard her pleas, if He cared, if He was going to get involved at all. She began to feel that even God had left her alone. If she couldn't get help from God, then she truly had nowhere to turn.

RED FLAG: *Do you lack a close friend or two who know the truth about your life?* ≷

Audrey wanted to believe that God cared. She continued to teach Bible studies and lead a small women's prayer group. She kept up her Christian faith in front of everyone around her, but inside she wondered if God cared at all. Maybe all that stuff she kept spouting about how God would intervene in people's most dire problems—maybe that wasn't true at all.

One thing she did know—divorce was out of the question. God had made that clear in Scripture. Besides, maybe their dad wasn't around much, but she couldn't imagine the looks on her teenagers' faces if she were to tell them about a divorce. She didn't want to put her children through that. She didn't want to think about shuttling them between families for holidays. Neither did she want to put her husband through that kind of embarrassment. It just wouldn't be worth it. She'd take her loneliness over destroying her family.

But loneliness was having its own devastating effects. She found herself desperate for any kind of attention and became obsessed with getting it. She had always worked out and watched what she ate. Now she began to dress in more sensual ways. She told herself it was for John, but really, she just hoped to be noticed.

Audrey was invited to speak to a women's group in another state, and on that trip it occurred to her that it would be so easy to also create speaking engagements that she didn't have. John didn't check up on her; he trusted her and was busy enough with his own schedule. Audrey began traveling out of state regularly, where she would take off her wedding ring and spend an evening at an upscale bar getting hit on by all kinds of men.

The deceit of her new lifestyle only added to the excitement. She had created an elaborate alternate persona—a persona that demanded more cover-up and lies with each new day. Audrey told herself that she could step out of her fantasy life at any time, but in truth she was addicted to the excitement of the game.

One cloudy morning, however, Audrey found herself in a hotel room, having broken her wedding vows and full of guilt and shame. Her life had spun out of control. She was a Christian. She knew better. How had it come to this? The man she'd slept with was already gone, but intense guilt settled over her like a thick blanket.

Audrey slowly showered and dressed, but she couldn't do anything about how dirty she felt. One thing she knew for sure—this was the last time she would lie to her family and sneak off on a fantasy trip. She had never intended it to go this far. She would go back to her lonely life. At least that wasn't filled with guilt and the awful possibility of being found out. For now, no one would ever know what had happened. ■

RED FLAG: *Do you refuse to allow your friends to be "real" with you, or do you need to see them as more or better than they are?* ≣

To this day, John does not know what Audrey did, and he remains unaware that his wife is unhappy. Audrey is a ticking time bomb. She struggles with depression and anxiety. Worse is the fact that she insists on carrying this burden alone. "No one can ever know," she insists to herself. She can't talk to any pastor in town—they all know her and her husband as exemplary Christians. She won't go to counseling because she knows her husband wouldn't have any patience for a wife having such difficulty. "Just shape up and pray about it!" he'd say. There is no time in his schedule for a depressed wife.

Problem is, she doesn't want to pray anymore. She's done praying. She prayed for years with no results. After what she's done, she doesn't want to face God or ask Him for anything. So she bears her secret alone—and slowly dies inside.

Because her husband's work is Christian work, Audrey felt she could not challenge his over-involvement. Like many involved in helping professions and in religious work, John found it difficult to see that his connection to his work took precedence over his relationship with Audrey and his children. Often a cause or a "call" seems so much more important than a wife or children with ordinary problems! Christian work can be very satisfying and time consuming and can meet deep needs. John chose to meet his needs through his work and refused to see the price his family paid for his absence.

A large red flag in John's life is his refusal to be accountable to other men. A healthy lifestyle for anyone involves having friends or mentors who can be trusted with the truth, not the public image. John is unwilling to cultivate those relationships.

The people who knew John and Audrey saw an idealized Christian leader and a perfect family, and Audrey did not feel she could expect support for her own needs from anyone she knew. John and Audrey were placed on a pedestal as exemplary Christian leaders, and no close friends were allowed to see what was happening behind their carefully maintained image.

So Audrey was caught in a double bind. If she told the truth to someone outside her family about how unhappy and lonely she was and that her marriage was in trouble, she would have the opportunity to get help, but she would feel disloyal to her husband. If she continued to do what she had always done and support her husband publicly, she would continue to live privately in loneliness and despair. And John was adept at causing her to think that the problem was all hers and that she needed to be more spiritual—"pray about it"—rather than get outside help.

But Audrey and John need help. Painful as it would be, if John remains unyielding after several repeated attempts by Audrey to draw his attention to the problems in their marriage, Audrey needs to involve someone else in the process. If she seeks the help of a licensed counselor, by the ethics of the profession the process would be confidential. That confidentiality would not be breached unless the counselor thought Audrey would harm herself or someone else or if Audrey told her of abuse occurring to someone under age eighteen. Even if John refuses to get help, Audrey needs to get support for herself as she tries to decide what she needs to do to address the problems in her marriage.

We were not created to live life alone, but in community. Audrey desperately needs friends she can confide in who will come alongside and support her as she deals with her unhappiness in her marriage and the guilt of her affair. "A ticking time bomb" describes Audrey accurately. By closing the door to her secret life, by getting no help and finding no ways to deal with her pain and unmet needs, Audrey is increasingly vulnerable to making more unwise choices in the future. By refusing to get help, she actually is reinforcing her own perception that she is not worth caring for and protecting!

THE TRUTH

Our life choices change us. We are not like dry-erase boards; we can't write a message on our lives one day and wipe it away the next. Our choices are more like drops of food coloring that enter the substance of our lives. We are impacted by what we do and by what we think.

"No one will ever know, I can end this anytime" is a lie for several reasons. First, when you are unfaithful, two people do immediately know—you know and your partner knows. Maintaining a secret life is an enormous burden in terms of energy and guilt. Second, continuing to keep the sin a secret does not always work, despite your best efforts. And when the secret becomes known, no one can predict the damage that will be caused. Third, putting a stop to a sinful behavior can be like trying to break free of an addiction—often, you are caught in your behavior and you *cannot* stop. And even if the affair and the behavior are ended, the impact of them on your thoughts and feelings persists.

The three women in the stories in this chapter each had very different life circumstances, but all were alike in that none of them *planned* to have an affair. Each opened herself up to temptation by minimizing the importance of her thoughts and then of the choices she was making. Imagine how different their lives would have been if they had been able to redirect their thoughts before acting on them!

We are more interconnected to others than we are aware, and our lives have the power to deeply influence other people. The well-loved movie classic *It's a Wonderful Life* shows the effect of this truth. Imagine your life right now as it impacts others. Think of the relationships that you currently have—with spouse, family, friends, neighbors, and coworkers. Think of the many people who know you and identify you with the cause of Christ. Think how those relationships would be impacted if you acted right now on some of the temptations you have faced.

One of the difficult realities of temptation is that we never know when we will be tempted or what form it will take. Just as an athlete stays in shape physically because she never knows when the competition will require extra reserves of strength, so healthy followers of Christ stay in shape mentally and spiritually because they never know when they will need to fight an unexpected battle against evil. The reverse of this principle is that when you give the enemy ground, you weaken yourself; when new temptations present themselves, you may not able to resist them.

The truth is that you have an enemy, Satan. He wants to bring you down. He doesn't want you to have a healthy, happy marriage. And he will provide plenty of temptation, both directly and indirectly, to get you to follow his plan instead of God's.

And the truth is that we make it easy for ourselves to *be* tempted. Are your activities setting you up for temptation? You may need to change your activities to protect your thought life. What you read, what you watch, and who you spend time with are all-important decisions that you make on a daily basis. Why spend your time walking the mall if you are trying to control your spending or struggling to honor God with your finances? Why cruise an online dating site if you want to honor your marriage vows? "Each one is tempted when, by his own evil desire, he is dragged away and enticed. Then, after desire has conceived, it gives birth to sin" (James 1:14–15).

How have you relied on spiritual disciplines to renew your mind? One helpful way to do this is to write down verses of Scripture that meet the needs you are currently experiencing in your life. When you are tempted to worry, to doubt, to question, or to covet, having verses available to read and repeat can be a powerful way to shift your thinking to God's truth about your situation.

Sometimes we, like Eve in the Garden of Eden, focus on the one thing we cannot have rather than delighting ourselves in the beauty and provision that God has already given or wants to make for us. Knowing what God's Word says about our value to our Father and His desire to give us real life is the best way to stand firm when temptations come. "May you experience the love of Christ, though it is too great to understand fully. Then you will be made complete with all the fullness of life and power that comes from God" (Ephesians 3:19, NLT).

take action

✓ Do you regard your thought life as under your control? Why or why not? If not, what will you do about it?

✓ How can you rely on spiritual disciplines to renew your mind?

✓ Go through this book again and write out the Scriptures from each chapter on small cards to carry with you at all times.

✓ Take some time to review the boundaries you have set for yourself to safeguard your own well being, your marriage, and your family. Are there ways that your activities are setting you up for temptation?

✓ What are some positive things you can do to increase your sense of well-being?

Conclusion

Hold On to Hope

The preceding stories are sobering and painful. You may have noticed a thread running through them all, a unifying theme. In each story, the woman was tempted and made the choice to walk a path outside of God's clear plan for our lives. By sharing these stories with you, I hope that you have been able to understand how Satan presents his lies to entice different kinds of women in different life situations. Each of these women believed a lie—and most of them acted on their belief. And now you know what happened as a result of their choices.

Perhaps you are also struggling, believing one of these lies about infidelity. Or perhaps there is a lie that you are struggling with that was not covered in these stories. In either case, I hope this book has caused you to reflect on the circumstances of your life with a clearer perspective so that you can avoid making these women's mistakes. One of Satan's cleverest deceptions is to make us think we can choose an evil course of action and not face consequences. He whispers that *you'll* be the one to get away with it. *You'll* be the one for whom everything will work out just fine. The painful truths of these stories expose that lie.

Sometimes Satan comes at us with the same temptation Eve experienced (which you read about in the Introduction), trying to get us to doubt God's wisdom and to convince us that we deserve more than God is currently providing. Perhaps you've had this experience: You're watching a movie about a woman caught in a desperate marriage. Along comes another man (a deftly chosen, very handsome and likeable actor) who can rescue her from her pain and take her away to a much better relationship. Isn't it intriguing how you find yourself cheering for the woman to leave her husband and to go off with her handsome lover? After all, the new man is providing her with the love that she hasn't received in her marriage. We *want* her to be rescued from her pain and to live happily ever after. It's amazing how susceptible we are to siding with a lie, especially when it's embedded in a story that's been written with a happy ending.

WHAT WILL YOUR LIFE STORY BE?

Through reading the stories of the women in this book and reflecting upon the truth, you have seen what Satan tries to do in our lives—but now what? What about the story of *your* life? How do you consistently resist temptation? How do you return to the Lord after you have sinned? How do you help a friend or someone close to you who is struggling?

When I face these questions, I am reminded what a great God we serve and what incredible power there is in the gospel! I am writing the conclusion to this book on Good Friday afternoon, the day when Jesus died on the cross for our sins, the day it seemed as if the evil one had won and the Son of God had been defeated. But in two more days, I will celebrate Jesus' resurrection. Satan did *not* triumph; Easter is coming! We need to be constantly reminded of the reality of Easter when the darkness of our lives is intense, when our relationships are damaged—sometimes beyond repair—and in need of the divine miracle of resurrection.

We need the hope of Easter whether we are convicted of our own sin or bearing the consequences of the sin of others. It is very hard to hold onto hope when life is falling apart, but remember—Easter is coming. God continues to work in our lives even when we fail Him, continues to love us even when we betray Him, and continues to be faithful to us even when we have been unfaithful. God is with us. He promises to make all things new (see Revelation 21:5). Through the Holy Spirit in us, we have the resources to resist sin, to be forgiven of our sins, and to return to the Lord in newness of life (see Romans 6:4)!

FINDING THE WILL TO RESIST

The surest way to resist temptation and to confront the lies of the evil one is to follow Jesus' example when He was tempted in the desert (you can read the story in Matthew 4:1–11). Jesus did not succumb to Satan's reasoning, nor did He try to resist Satan's lies with arguments; instead, he clearly spoke God's Word. Even when Satan turned the tables and quoted Scripture for his own purposes, Jesus still persisted in standing for the truth and speaking the Word of God correctly.

To use God's Word in this way, we need to know it and be able to confront our own thoughts with the truth of Scripture. We need to preach the gospel to ourselves to remain true to our Lord.

Sometimes women who are contemplating marital unfaithfulness or are already caught in it try to use Scripture to justify their actions. They rationalize that no matter what they do, God will still forgive them, or that God would want them to be joyful. They say that they have never felt so alive as they have in their affair. This new man's love has changed their lives—something that brings so much positive feeling must be God's will, right?

Realize that sin is fundamentally disorienting and that even the message of God's love can be distorted. If this is your situation, I encourage you to pray David's prayer in Psalm 139:23–24:

Search me, O God, and know my heart;
test me and know my anxious thoughts.
See if there is any offensive way in me,
and lead me in the way everlasting.

David realized that he needed God to search his heart. He knew he could not rely on his human understanding but had to be dependent upon the Lord's wisdom and insight. God will do this for us today as we present our hearts and souls to Him for His scrutiny, guidance, and grace. If we submit ourselves to Him, He will reveal to us the ways that we need to change and grow.

If you have a friend who is contemplating or is already moving toward a sinful relationship, do not hesitate to tell her gently what you see. Pray for the right attitude and the timing to do so, and definitely speak from a position of tenderness and respect, not in judgment or condemnation. Speak as someone who could also be tempted and would want a friend to extend the same love and care to you. Choose your words carefully, and don't feel as if everything has to be said in one conversation. Often a few well-chosen words can work more effectively than a lengthy lecture that can easily be blocked out!

I hope for all of us that we would have such friends in our lives who could so speak the truth to us in love. We need to develop friendships where this is possible and where others do not hesitate to tell us when they see our lives going off course. My experience has been that few people do this delicate work without second-guessing themselves about how much to say or even wondering if they should say anything. A good test is to ask yourself, "If I were in a similar situation, how would I want to be treated?" and then act accordingly. Sometimes a few words are all that is needed to help a friend become aware of future consequences and to spare her a great deal of pain.

THERE IS HOPE

If you have read these stories from the painful vantage point of knowing firsthand the damage that an affair can do, I want to encourage you again that there is hope. God stands ready to forgive us at the moment we confess our sins to Him. His forgiveness is complete. "So now there is no condemnation for those who belong to Christ Jesus" (Romans 8:1, NLT). Even though you may have to walk through the pain of the consequences of your actions, know that God will walk with you and give you the grace, like manna, that you need to survive each day.

I also want to encourage you to get help for this journey. You need not bear the burden alone. Find a pastor or counselor whom you trust to give you guidance. Seek out a group of believers who will extend God's grace and forgiveness to you, and make yourself accountable to them as the Holy Spirit does His healing work in your life. Jesus' words to the woman caught in adultery ring true for us today: "Go and sin no more" (John 8:11, NKJV). Healing is a process; it will take time for your feelings and thoughts to match up with what you know is right. There may be weeks or even months where you are obedient but you still struggle with thoughts and feelings for the other person. Like breaking an addiction, this kind of battle is hard to fight alone. Finding friends to encourage you, stand with you, and pray for you can make all the difference!

The apostle Peter is an example of someone who betrayed a person he loved but then was forgiven and restored. Jesus knew Peter would fail Him at a crucial moment, and even told him ahead of time that Satan had asked to "sift you as wheat" (Luke 22:31). Satan was given permission, but listen to Jesus' words: "But I have prayed for you, Simon [Peter], that your faith may not fail. And when you have turned back, strengthen your brothers" (Luke 22:32).

Peter did fail when he denied three times that he even knew Jesus! But Peter repented of his sin and was forgiven and restored (see John 21). Peter returned to God and through God's work in his life became an even stronger warrior for God's kingdom. He understood about temptation, sin, failure, and so he was able to help others heading in that same direction. While there are consequences for our actions, God uses our brokenness and humility as we again offer our lives to Him. We are a forgiven people, and certainly it is possible for God to use our healed and healing wounds for His glory.

If you've failed, turn back to God. Accept the consequences, ask for strength to bear them, seek restoration if possible, and ask God to use your brokenness to help you strengthen your Christian sisters.

One of my favorite verses is 2 Timothy 1:7: "For God did not give us a spirit of timidity, but a spirit of power, of love and of self-discipline." Satan is a defeated foe, and God, through His work in our lives, has given us the power to resist evil. As Moses told Joshua, "Be strong and courageous" (Joshua 1:6). Affairs are not inevitable, even when marital problems are intense. Through God's empowering help, you can walk in a way that pleases Him and resist temptation.

FINDING VICTORY

Just as the Bible records temptations and stories of failure (I told you several of these in the Introduction), it also records victories through God's enabling and mighty power.

Abigail's story describes a woman in difficult circumstances who lived fully for God (see 1 Samuel 25). Abigail's circumstances were not happy. She is described as an intelligent and beautiful woman who was married to a surly, self-centered man. The Bible calls her husband, Nabal, a fool. Abigail certainly had reasons to leave her husband. Surely God would not want her to stay with such a wicked man! How could she live out her faith in a way that honored God while under the authority of a fool?

Yet Abigail persisted, remaining in a marriage that was far from her dream come true. She lived in such a way that she was ready to act immediately to save her household from her husband's poor judgment. Abigail was able to honor God with her life, even in the middle of a marriage to an evil man. Abigail has always fascinated me by her willingness to act independently of her husband even as she was faithful to him. The lesson of her life is not to passively accept whatever circumstances you find yourself in, but to make godly choices in the midst of those circumstances. Through her quick action, resourcefulness, and attunement to God's will and plan, Abigail averted disaster not only for Nabal and her household but also for David.

Mary, Jesus' mother, is another woman who obeyed God in the midst of difficult circumstances. As a virgin, she was asked to be the mother of God's Son—the situation was replete with opportunity for misunderstanding and judgment by everyone around her. Yet Mary didn't argue or worry because this wasn't the way she wanted her life to be. She submitted her own dreams to God's will and plan, and she replied to the angel, "May it be to me as you have said" (Luke 1:38). Mary had the courage to fully trust God. Our obedience to God's plan usually must precede knowing exactly what that is in its entirety!

Sometimes we have the mistaken view that God cannot use our lives when they have been marred by someone else's sin. Hagar bore a child by another woman's husband, through no choice of her own. Then she was rejected by that man (who, incidentally, was Abraham; see the story in Genesis 16). As a single mother, Hagar was forced to wander in the desert with her son, Ishmael. But she cried out to God, and He answered her. When no one else saw her desperate circumstances, her pain, and her suffering, God saw and delivered her. In the day-to-day struggle of our lives, often God is the only one who sees. But He sees, He answers, and He gives us strength to walk some incredibly difficult paths.

THE CHOICE IS YOURS

As a counselor, one of the privileges I have is to come alongside individuals in very stressful life circumstances. (Yes, I *do* see that as a privilege!) I am often amazed by the capacity people have to make very difficult godly choices in the midst of painful life circumstances. In his book on suffering, *Man's Search for Meaning*, Victor Frankel, a concentration camp survivor, wrote that we cannot choose our circumstances but we can choose our response to them. In journeying with others through suffering, I have seen many private acts of heroism. Again I am reminded of the God who sees.

I do not know your life circumstances, but it is my prayer that this book will give you insight and courage. Take heart! Know that some of your greatest victories may not be seen by others, but they *will* be witnessed only by God. You can never predict the positive impact of resisting temptation or repenting of sin and then continuing to choose to follow God. May you continue to find your deep strength and comfort in Him as you run the race He has laid out for you. He walks with you through the most desperate times and promises to bring you out on the other side. To God be the glory!